M000106363

'033
792

PREVAIL

Celebrate the Journey

ALDER ALLENSWORTH

Published by Richter Publishing LLC www.richterpublishing.com

Editors: Monica SanNicolas, Margarita Martinez, Natalie Meyer

Proofreader: Nastassia Clarke

ISBN:194581232X
ISBN-13:9781945812323

DISCLAIMER

This book is designed to provide information on sailing and cancer. This information is provided and sold with the knowledge that the publisher and author do not offer any legal or medical advice. In the case of a need for any such expertise, consult with the appropriate professional. This book does not contain all information available on the subject. This book has not been created to be specific to any individual's or organization's situation or needs. Every effort has been made to make this book as accurate as possible. However, there may be typographical and/ or content errors. Therefore, this book should serve only as a general guide and not as the ultimate source of subject information. This book contains information that might be dated and is intended only to educate and entertain. The author and publisher shall have no liability or responsibility to any person or entity regarding any loss or damage incurred, or alleged to have incurred, directly or indirectly, by the information contained in this book. You hereby agree to be bound by this disclaimer or you may return this book within the guarantee time period for a full refund. In the interest of full disclosure, this book contains affiliate links that might pay the author or publisher a commission upon any purchase from the company. While the author and publisher take no responsibility for the business practices of these companies and or the performance of any product or service, the author or publisher has used the product or service and makes a recommendation in good faith based on that experience. Most characters appearing in this work have given permission. As this journey occurred close to twenty years ago it was impossible to contact all those involved. The names of some characters and organizations have been retained, others have been changed to protect their identity. Any other resemblance to real persons, living or dead, is purely coincidental. This story is the opinion of the author and not that of the publisher.

DEDICATION

This book is dedicated to the memory of my father,
Thomas M. Allensworth, Jr. Dad taught me to sail and to treat all people
with respect. He provided me with the opportunity to write this book.

CONTENTS

ACKNOWLEDGMENTS

I would like to first thank the Sailability volunteers and the sailing community of greater Tampa Bay, who joined together in the mission of making our waters accessible to all. Without these fine people, the *Prevail* trip would have been meaningless and Sailability Greater Tampa Bay would have never left the dock. Although these people are too numerous to mention by name (and I wish I could), each one holds a special place in my heart.

I would like to thank Richter Publishing for giving me the opportunity to compete in and win their 2017 writing contest. This opportunity has led to the publishing of this book and the telling of a very special story. I could not done it without them.

I would also like to thank Peter and Sharron Childs for reading my first draft, making lots of wonderful suggestions, and encouraging me to submit the manuscript to the contest.

Tom Casey was an incredible unwavering support throughout the sail and continues to be now as a friend. I would like to thank all the sponsors for making this trip possible, and Chris Bauer for building such a sweet little boat.

I would like to thank Chris Mitchell for building the Access Dinghy and taking a risk on a bunch of volunteers to start Sailability Greater Tampa Bay. I especially would like to thank Daniel Davison for his support of the trip and for supporting the inception of Sailability Greater Tampa Bay, Inc. I am grateful to Tim Wall and CNN for feeling as though this trip was newsworthy and for filming the voyage and airing it on *American Voices*.

I would like to thank my father and mother for sticking by my side through all my health issues and my adventurous endeavors.

Lastly, I would like to thank my husband, Ben Ritter. I met him through the founding of Sailability and he has been an integral part of the complete process.

PROLOGUE

To whom much is given, much is required -
not expected, but required.
~

- Andrew Young -

According to CNN anchor Leon Harris, "You have to be out of your mind to board a 12-foot boat and then set out on a 2000-mile odyssey, but that's exactly what 42-year-old cancer survivor Alder Allensworth did."

Was I out of my mind for embarking on such an odyssey? No. In actuality, I had been unknowingly preparing for that moment my whole life.

When the Sailing Program for People with Disabilities (SPPD) asked me to sail a 12-foot boat from St. Petersburg, Florida to Camden, Maine, I knew it was the right thing to do. What an incredible opportunity! Sailing was my sanctuary, my place of healing. Now, I had the opportunity to share sailing with the world.

However, sometimes the reality of an offered and accepted opportunity is a bit different from the actual execution.

The CNN cameras caught me as I yelled, "Slow down, your wake!" as yet another powerboat came blasting past, splashing water all over me and into the boat. I also yelled a few other choice words, which I won't repeat in print. I'm a sailor, and have been known to have the vocabulary of one.

I stretched my arm out and moved it up and down, the waterskiing sign for *slow down*. The guy just waved at me as he reached for his cocktail, squeezed his bikini-clad crew, and disappeared down the waterway. I quickly turned the tiller and grabbed the mainsheet so I could maneuver and take the wake at a 45-degree angle to minimize the chance of capsizing and the amount of water being thrown into the boat.

I replayed this scene again and again for hours on end as I made my way north up the Intracoastal Waterway.

How did I come to find myself in this horrible state, constantly

1

changing my course to avoid serious injury or even death?

In 1990, at 33 years old, I was diagnosed with an extremely rare cancer, adenoid cystic carcinoma (ACC) of the lacrimal (tear) gland. I was case number 80 documented in the world, and according to my doctors, no one had ever survived. When I was diagnosed, the cancer was so rare, there was no one else that I could talk to with the same diagnosis. There was no Facebook, and email was in its infancy.

Now, 27 years later, resources have increased and it's easier to connect to others who have ACC. There are many strains of this disease, depending on which part of the body is affected. About seven years ago, a friend asked me if I had yet to meet anyone with the same diagnosis. I found the Facebook page and became connected.

Research into ACC is sparse because this is an "orphan disease." This means there are too few people affected by it to warrant significant research funding. Both the Adenoid Cystic Carcinoma Research Foundation and the Adenoid Cystic Carcinoma Organization International provide support and hold fund raisers to assist people who are diagnosed with this disease. (See website links in References and Resources Section.) My hope is to inspire people with a devastating diagnosis to live fully and to focus on their abilities, not their disabilities.

This is the story of my journey, my remedies, and the treatments I personally sought. The interpretation and experience are mine alone. This means there are no guarantees. People have asked me for my story and how I survived an unsurvivable cancer. Here is that story.

It could be just good luck, good karma, or maybe it wasn't my time. Maybe it was one of the many things I did for self-care, or a combination of all of them. If there is something to take away from this book, it's that I made a decision to live despite the cancer. I also accepted that one day I would die. I refused to live in fear of death. That doesn't mean I haven't had my despairing moments, but I chose to live in joy and not let cancer control my life or my decisions.

None of us know when we are going to die or what is going to kill us. We cannot live in fear; this is NOT living. Yes, sometimes I felt miserable, with the cancer overshadowing everything else, but I was blessed not to have many down days. When I did have one, my friends and my passion for sailing lifted me up.

One of my pet peeves is when someone says "my cancer" or a medical professional, friend, or family member says "their cancer" or "Sally's cancer." This possessiveness when it comes to cancer makes my skin crawl. My belief is don't own the stuff and don't label someone with it. When we use possessive terms such as "my" or "their," we imply ownership. I don't want to own the cancer.

When I talk about someone who has been diagnosed with cancer, I say "the cancer." I don't want to imply any kind of ownership or guilt trip a person into thinking they created it. I have seen the courage of those diagnosed on Facebook, living despite the cancer. People are people, not the diagnosis.

The kindest thing I heard when I was undergoing the surgery to eradicate the cancer came from a young resident: "I am so sorry. What bad luck."

I needed to hear that it was not my fault; it was just plain bad luck. This really relieved any feelings of guilt and gave me permission to go beyond the diagnosis.

CHAPTER 1

Without hope there can be no faith; without faith in the world and in yourself there can be no true love, no real compassion; and without compassion there can be no future.

~

- Tristan Jones -

This journey began in the spring of 1990. I was finishing up my master's degree and I was exhausted; I worked full-time and had a 90-mile commute to school. I had a bad case of the flu that was giving me vertigo. My cousin drove me to the doctor and a wonderful nurse practitioner asked me why my eye was drooping. I told her I was exhausted from spending too many hours on the road and in front of a computer, but she shook her head, not buying it. She gave me a prescription for the vertigo, a symptom of the flu, and set me up to see an ophthalmologist.

I showed the ophthalmologist a small lump, about the size of a pencil eraser, protruding from under my left eyebrow. I'd just recently started to notice it when putting on mascara. The ophthalmologist suggested an infected lacrimal gland and put me on a round of antibiotics. While I really appreciated trying a non-invasive treatment first, nothing changed; the lump was still there and the eyelid continued to droop.

The ophthalmologist then suggested an MRI of the head to determine what was going on. The results came back: a tumor around the lacrimal gland. The doctor was quite matter-of-fact and positive when he said most of these are benign (not cancerous), but said that I should still have it removed. My heart stopped for a moment when he said the word "tumor," but I grabbed onto his reassurance that it was probably benign, like a drowning person being thrown a life-ring. He sent me to a surgeon.

It was May, and I was getting ready to graduate. So, while others were walking across the stage, I was spending the night in the hospital. It was supposed to be a quick, easy surgery, with just a 24-hour hospital stay. The surgeon warned me that if the tumor had infiltrated the eyelid, he would have to remove it.

On hearing that, I had a flash of my grandfather's face. He'd had skin cancer from years of working in a creosote plant in the sun, and he'd had to get an eyelid removed. As a result, that eye always ran tears. It didn't bother him vanity-wise, but he was old. I was 33. The thought of that disfigurement was almost more than I could handle.

When I woke up from the surgery, the surgeon said they'd only removed the tumor and had left everything else intact. What a relief; I still had eyelids and eyelashes. I still had my face.

My parents and I had a conference with the surgeon that I don't remember much about. My parents told me the surgeon said he had never seen anything like this tumor before and believed it could be malignant (cancerous). He had removed the grape-sized tumor encapsulating my lacrimal gland and sent it to M.D. Anderson for pathology. It turned out that was (and is) the best place in the world for diagnosing lacrimal gland tumors.

To this day, I still do not remember him saying the tumor was malignant. This lack of memory could fall into the category of still feeling the effects of the anesthesia or denial; most likely denial. Denial is a defense mechanism we use when we're not able to cope with something, so we deny it's happening. In some cases, it can be very self-destructive—such as with addictions—but in other cases, it's very useful. Our brains don't allow the information into our consciousness because we can't emotionally handle it yet. Once we get to the point of being able to handle the information, then it becomes accessible. Amazing how our brains work.

I sent my parents home and told them I was fine. The tumor was out, and I had a brand-new master's degree. Time to have some fun in life and get to sailing! I had bought an old boat to refurbish and now was the time.

Having read that crystals and meditation are wonderful healing tools, I decided to accelerate the healing of the surgical incision with a crystal on the surface of the wound while meditating. I would do this a couple of times a day, focusing the meditation on healing, using my subconscious to start the healing process even though my conscious mind had not grasped the reality that I had been diagnosed with cancer. Our brains are wondrous things. The way we can compartmentalize to survive shock, yet continue to function, to survive and even thrive is brilliant.

One day I was lying on the couch in the living room, meditating with the crystal on the incision. All of a sudden, I felt something warm running down my face. I got up and went to the bathroom. Blood was squirting out of the incision with each pump of my heart.

I grabbed a towel and put pressure on the wound, then called the emergency number for the doctor and they talked me through putting ice on the wound and seeing if I could slow the bleeding before I made a trip to the ER. The bleeding did slow and eventually stop, so I didn't have to make a trip to the ER.

Sometimes you do get a bleeder after surgery; maybe that vessel had not been tied off very well. Maybe the power of the crystal was more than I realized and created too much blood flow and pressure. Maybe the bleeding was a cleansing of the area and releasing all cancer cells left behind. Maybe it was a combination of all three; I'll never know.

Several weeks later, just before Fourth of July weekend, I went in alone to get the results of the pathology. I was confident that everything was fine and I was ready to get on with my life. I had a crew of friends lined up to help me pull my sailboat out of the water in order to paint the bottom. I was excited to apply for a Ph.D. program in psychobiology. I had things to do.

I walked into the doctor's office and went to sign in at the desk. When the receptionist looked up and saw me, the color drained from her face. The other office staff turned as she said my name, and a look of pity and sadness crossed their faces.

The penny dropped, it was not good news. Nonverbal communication is powerful.

The doctor took me back right away and told me the tumor was malignant. He said he had never seen this kind of cancer before, and referred me to experts in this area. He was aware of one man, much older than I, who had lived for seven years after radical surgery and then died of something else. The doctor said he had made me an appointment (which he strongly suggested I keep) for later that day with a specialist in Ft. Lauderdale.

I numbly left his office and drove to the back entrance of the hospital where I worked, as I didn't know where else to go. I was employed as a music therapist, providing care to severely emotionally disturbed adolescents. It was an incredible long-term treatment program with a 98% success rate. The program was being threatened because of the advent of managed care. Insurance did not want to pay for long-term treatment even though it worked and saved money in the long run.

I went into the back where the staff offices were, away from the adolescents and knocked on Dr. Kelly, MD, the director's door. He let me in; he knew it was bad as soon as he saw my face.

I told him what I'd understood about what the doctor said. Dr. Kelly called in one of the nurses, and they figured out how to let another nurse, Eileen, who was a close friend, off so she could drive me to Ft. Lauderdale and be a second set of listening ears. The support I received from this treatment team to which I belonged was incredible.

We arrived at the doctor's office and I was given the usual paperwork to fill out with my medical history. Standard stuff, except this time I had to mark the square indicating that I had cancer. I sure didn't want to do it. My hand hesitated over the square. Did I really have cancer? I wasn't willing to accept it. If I marked the box, I had to admit that I had it. It was horrible, and not something I was even beginning to get my head wrapped around. Reluctantly I checked the box.

We were taken straight back to see the doctor. He started telling us about having been diagnosed with head cancer himself and who had done the surgery to remove the tumor. He then let me know I had a very bad, aggressive cancer and needed to be treated immediately. He said there were only two surgeons in the world who did the surgery I needed, and one was in London. The other, Dr. S. Anthony Wolfe in

Miami, was the best.

I figured Miami was closer than London, so the doctor called and set up an appointment for me the next day. Talk about the red-carpet treatment! I had never been treated so quickly and so well in a doctor's office; usually you had to wait until you were nearly a corpse.

We drove back to West Palm Beach, and Eileen suggested we call my parents and then go out to eat at this great little Italian place. My parents lived about three hours away and said they would be down in time for my afternoon appointment the next day. Eileen and I ordered dinner and wine, and I do believe the wine went down a lot easier than the dinner. I was glad I had a designated driver.

The next day, my parents and I headed to Miami. When we arrived at the office, the waiting room was full of people in different stages of facial surgery. It was a bit frightening to see some of them. I was taken aback when I got to see the doctor very quickly; more red carpet.

Dr. Wolfe didn't pull any punches, and said the whole eye and orbit had to come out as soon as possible. I struggled to grasp what this meant. My parents just sat there stoically. Dr. Wolfe took a medical book down from a shelf and opened to a page with a picture of a young man without an eye. That side of his face was just covered over with skin. It was horrible, I thought as I felt myself shutting down. The doctor said, "The side of your face will be a blank, just like this picture." The man's face *was* blank; there was no expression there whatsoever. Will I become that way, a zombie? I found no warm, fuzzy bedside manner there. Made me just want to sign up and have my perfectly good eye taken out, because of a tumor in my tear gland.

Really! I was ready to bolt. But I stayed bolted to my seat, frozen as if in a nightmare. Every day of delay meant a lower chance of living. He told me about a high-profile patient, a professional model, who'd had the same diagnosis. This patient did not want to lose the eye and went to the islands to try an alternative fruit treatment. That same patient died. I was told I had a week to decide, as this was the next opening in his surgical schedule. We filed out quietly and made the drive back to West Palm Beach.

Once home, we talked about resources. My father had worked with an admiral whose son married the daughter of the lacrimal gland pathologist at M.D. Anderson. What incredible synchronicity! He got on the phone immediately to see what he could find out.

My mom just looked at me and said, "I am so sorry I had you." Mom believed that she had passed on a "bad gene" that had created this disease and was apologizing for putting this experience on me, though she had no control over what genes I inherited.

I looked at her as waves of shock continued to course through my body. This had just happened; it wasn't her fault, and I was trying to understand what it meant. My deeper self took over and responded, "Thank you for my life."

Once those words were out, we hugged and cried. The day continued on, and somehow, we got through it. We made calls to my brothers to let them know. I made calls to my friends. I had some fun things lined up. It was almost the Fourth of July, and I had been invited to a party.

I called my boss and told him my options. He had attended medical school in Miami and started checking his sources. My best friend Shawn lived in Miami and worked close to the medical school, so she went to the medical library and asked them to pull information on the disease. They could not find very much information, and what they could find was all bad news.

The pathologist had a long conversation with my father. He said that I was case 80 documented in the world and no one had survived the disease. The only chance I had was to have anything affected by the cancer removed. He gave me a 10% chance to live, if I lived through the surgery. He confirmed what I'd been told before: there were only two surgeons in the world capable of this task, Dr. Wolfe in Miami and another surgeon in England.

This echoed the doctor I saw in Ft. Lauderdale. I like consistency, so surgery it was. The big day was scheduled for July 11. But there was still a lot of living to do before I lost my life.

I had to decide how I wanted the surgical wound to be repaired. Did I want the incision closed with a skin graft? Did I want metal snaps sticking through the skin to snap on a fake eye? Did I want to leave the cavity open so I could insert an acrylic plate with a prosthetic (fake) eye? None of these prostheses included a blinking or moving eye. It would be static. I could wear glasses to disguise the area so it didn't look so fake.

Since I'm an avid sailor and scuba diver, the site needed to be waterproof. I asked what the options were. It turned out that the most waterproof alternative would be to seal the wound with a skin graft. This was more important than vanity to me, so the decision was made: close it up with a skin graft. I could always do something different later if I changed my mind.

I had to get my "affairs" in order. Such an interesting word, "affairs." The particular meaning in this case is not pleasurable! I took care of legal items, such as power of attorney for finance, healthcare, and a will. My brothers came and we had some quiet walks on the beach, talking about life, death, beliefs, and saying goodbye. We cleaned, painted, and launched my sailboat.

I spent as much time as possible that week in the water, on the water, and by the water. I also spent time with my friends and co-workers. We had a big Fourth of July party and a heavily contested volleyball game. My mantra became, "I can play volleyball with one eye." The fireworks were incredible, but the support from friends and family surpassed them.

I got a call from my parents' church, which I attended every time I visited them. I was on the prayer list and they had then added my name to prayer lists all over the country. What an incredible feeling, knowing so many people were sending me healing energy.

Several years before, at a music therapy conference, I had attended a lecture by Dr. Larry Dossey, MD, about the power of prayer. He shared a double-blind study that had been done at a large inner-city hospital (Byrd, 1988). Every patient with cardiac disease who came into the emergency room was randomly selected via computer to either be on a prayer list or not. The first names of the patients being prayed for were sent to a wide variety of churches of all different denominations throughout the United States. The patients didn't know whether they were being prayed for, and the medical staff didn't know who was on what list.

It turned out that the patients who were prayed for did statistically better than those who were not. Incredible! Yes, put me on all the prayer lists available.

The week passed quickly by and it was time for surgery. I had to go in the day before for all the pre-op work. I was given a private room—nice!

After convincing the doctor to let me have a pass to go out to dinner, we went to my favorite restaurant in Miami, Shell's. The seafood was incredible, but the peanut butter chocolate pie was even better. We had a wonderful time—me, my brothers, my parents, and my best friend, Shawn.

My family took me back to the hospital and went on to their hotel, and Shawn came up to the room with me. She's an incredible person, one of my heroes. We were classmates and roommates while studying music therapy at the University of Missouri, Kansas City.

In 1985, Shawn contracted a virus that left her partially paralyzed from the neck down. Her parents were told to put her in a nursing home, but Shawn is stubborn. She was able to make it through rehab, get her own apartment, and a part-time job.

A couple of years later, we were at a music therapy conference and I sat next to a man who worked in the Veterans Administration (VA) Healthcare system. He told me about a job at the Miami VA for a music therapist. I told Shawn; she applied and was accepted. They would make accommodations for her. She took the job, moved to Miami, and found an apartment. She even went back to school and earned a master's degree.

Today, she has to use a wheelchair full-time to get around and has hand controls on her car, as her legs don't work very well. She also dances with a mixed ability troupe. She lives a full life.

Shawn gave me a necklace with a pendant of an elephant with its trunk up; a good luck piece. She said she knew I would come through this. I have always trusted Shawn's intuition. I walked with her to the elevator, as visiting hours were over.

A nurse came up to us, looked straight at Shawn, and said, "Visiting hours are over and you need to get to bed. I'll help you."

Shawn and I looked at each other and burst out laughing. Shawn said, "Got the wrong patient. I'm going home. She's the one who's staying."

The nurse had a stern look on her face; she was not going to put up with this kind of nonsense on her shift. I quickly jumped in and confessed to being the patient. Then I gave Shawn a hug and followed the nurse back toward my room. The nurse made a detour for some strong coffee and to the chart room, just to make sure we were telling the truth.

I went to my room, still laughing, and got ready for bed. The nurse came in then, apologized, and said I looked too healthy to be a patient. I could not have agreed more!

After I got settled into my room, a neurosurgeon who was part of my surgical team stopped by, and said that he believed I may be able to keep the eye. Hope sprang up in me and tears came to my eyes. It was easier to go to sleep that night than I'd expected it would be, now that I had this feeling of hope.

The next morning I was up early because Dr. Wolfe made a point of stopping by. He apologized for the mixed messages, and said that the neurosurgeon was wrong and the eye would still have to come out. When he saw the devastation on my face, he said, "Well, you know I don't like taking eyes out of pretty girls' faces. It's the only shot you have at life."

Crying, I got into the shower. I was going to have my eye taken out today. I could not wrap my head around it. The undeniable fact was that I could lose more than my eye today; I could lose my life. I realized I still had the elephant necklace on and as I went to take it off, it slipped out of my wet fingers, hit the tile floor, and shattered. Not a good omen. Tears started coming harder and faster, mixing with the water from the shower.

My family came in after this. I washed my face, put on the stylish hospital gown and a smile. I greeted them and they asked when I was going down to surgery. I didn't know. The nurse said she thought it would be a couple of hours' wait, as an emergency had come in and they needed the operating room.

My parents had brought a couple of decks of cards. My father was a Navy dentist, and we'd moved every couple of years as I was growing up. My parents enjoyed playing bridge. When my brother and I were old enough, they taught us to play. We would travel and play bridge as a family. It was one of the things that kept us together.

We'd played several hands that day, when I got a humdinger; I had 22 points and eight hearts with honors. My partner liked my hearts and supported me in the bid. For those non-bridge players, this is a rare hand, with great winning potential. I won the bid, and I was going to clean house. But the nurse and transport aid arrived to take me to surgery, so I never got to play that hand.

In pre-op, the anesthesiologist came in to do his assessment. I let him know pretty quickly that I had read the literature on people being able to process information while under anesthesia. It's an altered state of consciousness, not unlike hypnosis; a person can be very suggestible under anesthesia. He said he was aware of the research. He knew I hadn't had time to give blood prior to the operation, so he would give me the suggestion not to bleed. He knew that under hypnosis there is a possibility of our bodies being able to control bleeding. He said he also knew I loved to windsurf and as I was coming out of the anesthesia, he would talk to me about how much fun I was going to have windsurfing once I healed.

I was stunned and quite relieved. It was incredible. This really made me feel more positive going into the operating room.

***

Windsurfing has been my passion since 1980. I love to sail. My father introduced my brothers and me to the sport in 1976, when he was stationed in Charleston, South Carolina. He had bought a 23-foot sailboat and we had some great times sailing around Charleston Harbor. I was in college at the time and could not afford my own sailboat, so I turned to windsurfing instead. With windsurfing, I fell into a passionate lust that has lasted many years. Like anything worth doing, it takes time and energy to get the basics and is initially quite frustrating. But like a bike, once you get the balance figured out, you have it for life! There is something about skimming across the water free as a bird. When sailing on a windsurfer, every nuance of wind, sea, and body movement is felt; it's such an incredible feeling to be so directly connected to the planet. I loved to sail out to islands and explore new areas.

I also became involved in racing windsurfers, which was a very new sport at the time. I was living in the Midwest and the lakes and wind were awesome. There were plenty of opportunities to learn to race, and learning to race sharpened my skills as a sailor. I became quite sharp and competitive. In fact, I didn't recognize the mild-mannered, non-competitive pacifist I'd once believed myself to be. I became a vicious competitor and believe that the part of myself driven to do my best in windsurfing served me well throughout the surgical ordeal.

Windsurfing, 1984

***

My surgery took nine hours. They cut my scalp ear to ear, opened my skull, and took my face off. They took everything out on the left side of my face that might have come in contact with the cancer, including my optic nerve all the way back through the brain. Then they put it all back together using some extra skull bones and rearranging muscles and skin grafts to make sure the eye socket would not be soft, but hard in order to protect my brain. The skin grafts came from behind my ear, which ultimately hurt more than the orbit.

I came to as they were wheeling me down a corridor; from the gurney, it looked sort of like a tunnel. I saw my family and friends watching me go by on my way to the ICU. I called to my family, "I can play volleyball with one eye, and I want a chocolate milkshake." I was sent to the ICU, not because I was critical, but because the surgeon didn't trust the floor nurses with my care until I was alert enough to fend for myself. He had given me strict orders not to let anyone touch the bandages over my eye.

After being put in bed in the ICU, everything became a blur of vomiting, trying to sleep, being poked, and seeing visitors. I just wanted them all to leave me alone.

I hate the feeling of coming out of anesthesia; I avoid surgery like the plague. I can't believe someone would voluntarily put himself or herself through anesthesia for a non-essential procedure. For me, it's about control. I hate not being in control; I don't do amusement park rides for this reason. The other part is how lousy I feel. I hate it.

I hadn't felt lousy at all from the cancer, which was one of the reasons it was so hard to wrap my head around even having it. I was strong, fit, and healthy. I ate right, exercised, and maintained a great weight for my height. I did all the right things. How could I have gotten this devastating disease?

After about 24 hours, I was released from the ICU and sent to a regular floor. I had some clear fluid coming out of my nose; the doctors were afraid that I was leaking spinal fluid because my dura (the fluid-filled sac that encases the brain) had been compromised. By necessity, they had to puncture this sac during the surgery.

They wanted to do a spinal tap, but I convinced them to hold off for a day and see if it stopped. I told them I had allergies, so those could be causing the runny nose. I didn't want a spinal tap. I'm a chicken! When the doctors came in, I would spend the time inhaling through my nose and exhaling through my mouth. I didn't want anything coming out of my nose. The fluid stopped, and I never had to get a spinal tap. What a relief!

In the field of psychology, there's something called "dissociation," where you essentially disconnect somewhat from thoughts, memories, or even personal identity. It can be severe, such as multiple personality disorder, or mild, such as when you cannot control the urge to "sneak" cookies while on a diet, and your brain is shut down. You may find a definition on the Mental Health America website. The link is in the reference section at the end of the book.

I would say I fell into the mild category. My first name is Anne, but I have been called by my middle name, Alder, my whole life. I always correct people when they call me Anne, because I just don't answer to it. No one calls me Anne, and I forget it's even a part of me. I didn't tell the doctors or the nurses about this; I just let them call me Anne. That way, everything was happening to Anne and not Alder. It was a way of preserving "Alder."

Anne was losing part of her face and would be disfigured for the rest of her life. Anne could die of this disease. It was easier to let Anne take the fall. I could preserve Alder for wellness. It took me a while to realize I was doing this. I believe our minds are smarter and better at self-preservation than we give them credit for. Barbara Vine (1987) said, "The wonderful thing about the human mind is the way it copes when the worst happens."

It didn't take long before I was discharged from the hospital. I was young and healthy, so I bounced back quickly. I hadn't looked like a patient before this started, and I wasn't about to start looking like a patient now.

After about ten days of recuperation, it was time to have the staples removed from across the top of my head. It looked like I was wearing a metal headband, if you didn't look too closely. The doctors only shaved that inch of hair where a headband would go, so it would be easy to cover up as the hair filled back in.

I knew I would have to cover up the wound area where my eye had been with a patch, but didn't want any old black patch off the shelf. I created a patch on which I'd embroidered a windsurfer—a bit of vanity there, a bit of inspiration.

Once again, I was in the waiting room of horrors, with people in different stages of getting their faces repaired. I was now one of "them." It has always been interesting to me, as long as I have been working in the health care field, to notice that people, including health care professionals, call patients or people they really don't want to be like, "them." I have heard the elderly and the infirm referred to in this manner. It bothers me, but I have been guilty of it, too. We are "them."

It was finally my turn to head back to the doctor and get the staples and bandages removed. The nurse started to take the staples out of my scalp with a staple remover. Yes, they use a staple remover. Then, the nurse got called out of the room. We were hearing screams and hysteria coming from down the hall.

Things quieted down and the nurse came back. She said a woman had had a facelift and was freaking out. Apparently the woman had been told she would initially have some bruising and swelling, but would look great in a couple of weeks. The nurse was just shaking her head. I offered to go down and talk to the woman. We all burst out laughing.

The staples came out and the nurse started removing the bandages over my eye, or what use to be my eye. I didn't look. I couldn't look. I was quietly hysterical inside, or maybe numb. They honored my feelings. The doctor said everything was healing well and put the patch on where my eye used to be.

We drove home with me sporting my windsurfer eye patch. The next morning, my father suggested I look at my face first thing.

He said it was better to look in the morning and then to spend the rest of the day doing something different.

We went into the bathroom and I uncovered the area. He stood behind me to break my fall if I fainted, but I didn't faint. I took a quick glance, enough to satisfy my father, and put the patch back on. I was numb.

Taken by the office of Dr. S. Anthony Wolfe, after the removal of the bandages

CHAPTER 2

You alone must do it, but you can't do it alone.

~

- O. Hobart Mowrer -

My folks went home, and I went into recovery mode. I had to learn to drive again, but with one eye. Don't try this at home; it takes practice. Going from binocular vision to monocular vision is tough. This means no depth perception and no peripheral vision on the left side. I have to turn my head much further to check the blind spot on my left side. Cars appear to be coming faster and closer than they really are. As a result, I'm one of those annoying people who doesn't pull out into traffic when a person with normal vision would. I have to have a larger gap in the traffic.

I've learned to sneak my hand forward until I touch a glass on a table so I know where it is. Otherwise, on multiple occasions I have gone to reach for a drink and closed my hand over air. And yes, playing volleyball is not as easy as I thought it would be. I have come up under a ball with all my force and hit air even as the ball hits the ground in front of me. It's an adventure.

I also got good at not looking at the left side of my face. I was a contact lens wearer and would only look at my face when I didn't have the lens in my right eye. This would make it a bit blurry, and I could pretend that it was normal. One day though I noticed the skin peeling off of the skin graft where my eye use to be. It was sort of like how skin peels after a bad sunburn. They hadn't told me that was going to happen. After going through an ordeal like this, even a little thing can be alarming.

I told them about it when I went in for a checkup. The surgeon told me it was normal; there was nothing wrong with the graft. He also told me that the graft had shrunk more than expected and was pulling my eyebrow down into the space where my eye would be. He said this was easily fixed with another surgery and graft, and he would do it in two years, if I lived. How optimistic!

The other thing I was experiencing was tons of phone calls. For a while, it was great to be so loved. But sometimes the outpouring of love and support could be overwhelming, and I was already overwhelmed enough. I love the website "Caring Bridge" (www.caringbridge.org), and wish it had been invented when I was going through the cancer. A Caring Bridge page is set up by or for the person with a devastating disease. Family and friends are invited to join it. You can post updates and friends can leave you messages of inspiration.

Unfortunately, I had to answer every call and tell the story over and over again. It was exhausting. With Caring Bridge, I could have let all my friends and family know what was happening without having to answer every call.

Love and support come in many forms. They're all meant genuinely, but some come from a place of fear. Many people tried to tell me about sure-fire alternative cures. They had the silver bullet, but no hard research to back them up. Some tried to fix my face. "Did you see on TV the latest …"

Stop trying to fix me, I would scream inside. *Just love me the way I am!*

My friend Eileen had a good friend, Dave, in Martha's Vineyard who we had visited earlier that spring. I called and asked him if I could come back for a couple of weeks; I had to get away. I had to have time to myself. Dave said come, so I booked my flight. My aunt and her family live in Massachusetts, so I set aside time to visit them, too.

I had a great time at my aunt's house. We went hiking in the mountains, picked blueberries, and just relaxed. My cousin came up to me one day and said he was humbled by what I was going through and how I had such a positive attitude. He said he complained when the drive-thru didn't get his hamburger right. How could I be so positive having been through such a tough thing, including facing death?

I hadn't even thought about it. I was so busy enjoying life and healing, I hadn't had time to complain. I hadn't yet had time to grieve, either. I was keeping busy!

This would be a great time to discuss gratitude. It is so important to have an attitude of gratitude. Every morning before I get out of bed, I do a gratitude list, usually starting with, "I woke up this morning." It's a great attitude adjuster. This doesn't mean I don't have blue days. Sometimes I allow myself the luxury of self-pity, but I don't let myself stay there too long.

Our brains are very plastic. (Doidge, 2015) This means we can change them. If we allow our brains to stay in self-pity, then we start to make well-used paths in our synapses, like grooves in a record. Because these synapses are so well-used, our thoughts then default to self-pity. I want my groove of thoughts to default to positive, so I say my gratitudes frequently. I only allow the blues infrequently, when I just need a blue day!

People would say to me, "How could you make the decision to have your eye out? I could never do that."

When it's a choice of your eye or your life, the choice is pretty easy. None of us know what we would do in the circumstances until we're faced with them. I believe I'm not more courageous than the next person. I was faced with the decision and was forced into making it. I didn't go willingly, and would have loved some better options.

At this point, it was time to go to Martha's Vineyard. I spent my days walking in the woods and by the seashore. Dave took me to visit some of the sights. One night, we went out to a bar and ran into a friend of Dave's. All of us were drinking and enjoying the evening when the friend started hitting on me.

Okay. I have not written yet about how I felt as a single woman losing part of my face. Now is as good a time as ever. I was very concerned that I wouldn't be attractive. I was disfigured; I had cancer. As such, I wasn't a good candidate for a long-term relationship.

I would go out with female friends and see beautiful couples together, and I would get so jealous of the women, feeling that I would never be attractive again, no matter how much I covered up the scar with prosthetics, patches, or glasses. I was afraid to enter into a long-term relationship because I could be dead in a couple of years and I couldn't do that to any man. I couldn't make any promises.

But this guy was hitting on me. He was cute, wealthy, single, and not from my neighborhood. This was not going to be a long-term proposition. Though I was lying to myself, thinking it could be, deep inside I knew it was a vacation deal. I went home with him, and we had a glorious evening. He then wined and dined me for the rest of my vacation.

At one point, I asked him point blank, "Why me, with having cancer and my face like this?"

He said, "Cancer is not contagious, but AIDS is, and I know you don't have that."

How romantic. How devastating. Who was I kidding? I was lying to myself. He just wanted to have some good safe sex and I just wanted to know I was still attractive to men; good-looking, successful men. I was also glad that a man could see past my face and enjoy being with me.

Too quickly, it was time to go home. Though I'd enjoyed being in a world full of support and no responsibilities, I had a job and a life, and it was time to get back to it. I had to face the realities of living with a disfigured face and a horrible prognosis.

Sitting on the ferry back to Boston, I sobbed, unable to control the tears. Those days of recovery and recuperation would serve me well, I just didn't know it yet. I am forever grateful to Dave for giving me the opportunity.

***

Feeling strong enough to go back to work, I was looking forward to being with the adolescents (my patients), being productive, and making a positive difference in the lives of others. I wasn't worried about how the adolescents would react to me. They sent me the most incredible handmade get-well cards.

Many of the cards used a rainbow for decoration. Though I hadn't realized it, one of my favorite songs is "Somewhere over the Rainbow," and the adolescents had picked up on that during our music therapy sessions together. It's amazing the parts we show of ourselves of which we are not aware. I loved my job.

The outpouring of love, support, and hope from the adolescents just made my heart soar. These adolescents had faced tremendous challenges. They had been severely abused and neglected; some of their stories would make your hair curl. Yet they could reach out to me and send me such messages of hope. Incredible!

I called my boss and we agreed that I would start coming to work a couple of days a week and then increase the time as I felt able. In about two weeks, I was back to full-time. It was great to be able to go to work and not to have to go to school. I was getting involved in life again.

I signed up to attend a workshop in Ft. Lauderdale on cancer and music therapy. I could get continuing education credits for it and also see if there was something I could also apply to my own life. The cancer center where the workshop was held was state-of-the-art, with both traditional and complementary medical treatments.

During the music therapy lecture part, the therapist said, "I tell my patients I know how they feel."

I spontaneously replied, "Oh, you've had cancer also."

"Oh, no," he said. "I've had bad things happen to me, so I can relate to bad things that happen to people."

"But you can't relate to having had cancer," I probed further; I could feel my ire coming up.

"You don't have to have had cancer to know how it feels."

"I beg to differ. You don't know how it feels unless you walk in those shoes."

He tried to argue with me and I left the group. I still feel strongly about this today. It's interesting that in today's textbooks, they're teaching nurses NOT to say, "I know how you feel."

Yes, my reaction was validated. You can have empathy, but you don't know how someone else feels.

The other issue that came up for me in this group was the importance of being productive. Medical professionals encouraged me to apply for disability and take time off. I didn't resonate with that line of thinking. I needed to be productive. We're on this earth to help each other; I couldn't back off now.

I had no ill effects, wasn't feeling sick, and was strong both physically and mentally. Recovered from the surgery, it was time I got back to contributing to society.

* * *

Back to work. I was wearing glasses that had a mirrored film on them so I could see out, but no one could see my eyes. Neither the psychologists nor the adolescents believed this was a good idea. It's so important to see someone's eyes; the eyes are the window to the soul. If you can't see them, it's hard to trust the person you're with. Hollywood uses tough characters with mirrored sunglasses. Good for them—not good for a therapist.

So, I changed the lens to clear on the right side, but the lens frosted on the left side so the scar was covered up. It's important for me to wear glasses. I only have one eye left; I must protect it. When I was growing up, glasses were not sexy. Those of us who wore them were considered nerds. Sometimes when going out or wanting to look a little sexier, I would put a patch on and wear my contact lens in my good eye. I made patches that matched my outfits and got so many compliments; I was chic!

As I mentioned before, people were always trying to fix me. I received so many books on curing cancer, so I started to read them. The one that was most recommended was *Love, Medicine and Miracles*, by Dr. Bernie Siegel (1986). I hated that book. I had a feeling of guilt. Had I created the cancer? Was I mentally unbalanced?

Did I need to see a therapist? What did I need to do in order to undo the damage I had done to myself? Could I have cured the cancer myself through intense self-reflection and not had to lose the eye? Yes, I hated the book, but it did make me think.

I decided to see a therapist, so I called my insurance company and got a referral. She was a nice woman with a Ph.D. in psychology. She did a suicide assessment, even though I assured her I wasn't suicidal. I said I needed to explore my life and the reasons why I had developed this disease. I also needed assistance in coping with my disfigured face.

She apologized and said she couldn't see me under my insurance.

She said the only way she could provide therapy was if I was holding a knife to my throat. I've been around the mental health world for a long time and I knew that if I was holding a knife at my throat, I would be locked up before I could say "Jack Robinson." No way would I do that.

I didn't feel suicidal, either. I just wanted to make sure I was coping well. I wanted to uncover anything that was maybe causing me to manifest cancer, but that type of therapy wasn't covered by my insurance. How sad!

I talked to one of the psychologists at work about my dilemma. He offered to provide therapy at half of his regular rate as a professional courtesy. This was an incredible gift. He was so supportive and helped me to tap into my internal resources, the ones I had lost sight of because they were being overshadowed by the cancer.

Another thing I did was review the work of Dr. O. Carl Simonton, MD (1978). I learned about his work while working on my master's degree. Dr. Simonton used guided imagery to assist patients in eradicating the cancer in their bodies. He is no longer with us, but has left a legacy at the Simonton Cancer Center (https://www.simontoncenter.com/). One of the processes he developed was guiding patients to come up with an image to rid the body of cancer, playing that image through their minds, and feeling the image within their bodies.

The image that spoke to me most was the Mr. Clean White Tornado. I would visualize and feel the white tornado cleaning out my eye socket. I would do this multiple times a day, for just a minute or two. For example, if I was sitting at a stoplight, I would visualize the tornado cleaning out my eye socket, eradicating all the cancer. I could find lots of little idle moments where I could evoke the image, and it felt good to be actively doing something positive to eradicate the cancer! I was taking a proactive stance.

Years later, in 2009, I took a course from Donna Eden (2008) on energy medicine for women. It was given over several days and we were trained in the techniques of energy healing. Donna came up to me during one of the exercises and asked me to see her after class. I was wondering what I was doing wrong. It kind of felt like being called to the principal's office!

We set up a time and place to meet. Her initial question was, "What is that white spinning energy in your eye socket? I've never seen anything like it before."

I was shocked. I hadn't thought about the image in years! Donna Eden is one of those people who can see energy fields. She was born that way. I asked her to describe what she was seeing. We had never had a conversation before, and she certainly did not know that I'd had cancer, or anything about the image I had used to clean it out of my system.

She replied, "You know, a spinning white vortex. That's what it looks like."

I then told her the story of the cancer and the imagery. It was her turn to be shocked. She, like me, agreed it must have come from the imaging I had done for so long. It felt incredible to have actual physical evidence of the imagery and the result of keeping the area where the cancer was clean and free of any cells that could cause havoc again.

CHAPTER 3

A smooth sea never made a skillful mariner, neither do uninterrupted prosperity and success qualify for usefulness and happiness. The storms of adversity, like those of the ocean, rouse the faculties, and excite the invention, prudence, skill and fortitude of the voyager.

~

- Author Unknown -

After I was back at work full-time, there were some changes happening in the health care system. Insurance companies were implementing a system called "managed care." I didn't understand all the ins and outs, but I did see that my role was being expanded to other departments in the hospital because they wouldn't fund a full-time music therapist on the adolescent unit. I was sad to cut programs to these patients, but I was also excited about the challenge of serving different populations within the psychiatry department.

One day, I was called into the nurse manager's office. She closed the door and said they were cutting my position to part-time. I'd heard rumors, so I asked why. She said they didn't think I was emotionally ready to be working full-time again.

I asked her for evidence of this. I hadn't had any psychological testing, nor had I received any complaints about my job performance. Additionally, no counseling had been offered. She said she'd personally observed my emotional frailty. I asked her if she had a credential to allow her to make that kind of psychological assessment. I knew she didn't.

She hemmed and hawed and finally said, "We're putting you to part-time; just be happy you aren't being laid off." I said to lay me off; they would have to lay off the people who'd been hired after me in the department. I had seniority, and people hired after me should have been placed on part-time first. She again said I was being changed to part-time.

Part-time meant no health insurance. BINGO. The penny dropped. They didn't want an employee who had cancer because I could cost them a lot of money. The insurer we had also owned the hospital. I'll keep the name of the organization to myself, as it may have changed for the positive over the years.

I had been under the delusion that insurance and hospitals were about caring for patients and employees. At that point, I started to lose my wide-eyed idealist point of view of the world.

That summer, the Americans with Disabilities Act (ADA) had been passed and signed into law by President George H. W. Bush. In 1965, the Equal Employment Opportunity Act (EEO) had been signed into law. I read all the signs posted in the break room about my employee rights. I then wrote a letter to the CEO of the hospital, demanding my full-time job back, and citing the EEO. I said I had been discriminated against because I had a disability. Cancer falls into that category.

I said if my job was not restored within one week that I would initiate a lawsuit. Before the week was out, I was called into my supervisor's office and told that I'd been put back on a full-time schedule. I received no explanation other than that, and I did not push for one. I was grateful! I got my job back and started making plans for some life changes. Fighting this fight had diverted energy and anger from the disease.

Being diagnosed with cancer had hit on some of my control issues. I was a planner and always had contingency plans. I had my life organized and took care of my body by eating right, staying fit, keeping a positive attitude, and maintaining a strong spiritual foundation. How had this happened inside of me? My whole being had let me down.

I felt tainted and out of control, so it was important to find areas of control in my life that would put me back on an even keel. Winning my job back gave me a renewed sense of control over my life.

My friend Brenda was coming to Florida. She had sent me lots of positive energy before and during the operation. She and I had done our music therapy internships together in Kansas City, Missouri. Brenda and her fiancé Bob were bicycling around the United States. They'd sold almost everything, put the remainder in storage and left Iowa, went northeast to Maine, and then down the East Coast to visit me. On the way they got married in Washington, D.C. where Brenda presented at the annual music therapy conference taking place at that time. What incredible courage to take a journey like that.

As they were coming to West Palm Beach, we set up a get-together with Shawn and a trip to the Keys to swim with the dolphins. We then drove over to Naples to visit with another university friend.

Brenda had great faith in the human ability for self-healing. She shared with me that she had cured her nearsightedness and no longer needed glasses. She did not mean to point out a deficiency in my ability to heal myself, but I took her story personally. Maybe I could have healed myself of the cancer and wouldn't have needed to have my eye removed.

At the time, I was driving her to look for a store so she could buy cigarettes. I let her have it about the cigarettes. If she could cure her vision, she certainly could stop smoking. I was angry, and with later self-reflection, jealous! She was beautiful, enjoying an incredible adventure with her husband, and I was disfigured, possibly terminal, going nowhere.

Smoking had become, and still is, a huge pet peeve of mine. It causes cancer; the evidence is clear. Secondhand smoke causes cancer. Why would anyone do something intentionally that could cause such a devastating disease? But I know it's a really hard addiction to break, one of the toughest. After several attempts, Brenda quit smoking 14 years later. My friendship with Brenda survived the situation, and we're even closer friends today.

Other people did challenge my decision to have the eye out. They said there were many alternative healing methods I could have pursued. These comments sent me into periods of guilt. I had studied healing through music. Why couldn't I heal myself? Why did I have to rely on traditional western medicine? Weren't there gurus in India who got cut and could quickly heal the wound? There were many stories of faith healing. Did I not have enough faith?

As I tearfully explored these questions, I also studied healing techniques, which resonated with me, those I believed increased my chances of being totally cured of the cancer.

I also thought about the obstacles to self-healing. We, in our western society, are taught to depend upon doctors and medications from pharmaceutical companies to heal us. I had no examples of anyone I'd grown up with who had self-healed. My mother had encephalitis as a child and was left with some residual paralysis, bladder, and kidney problems. Dependent on doctors for treatment, she was never supportive of my pursuit of alternative healing methods. She was a scientist.

I know there are things that can make a positive difference, but these have not been aggressively studied by the medical profession because there's no money in it. Money is a big issue in the field of medicine.

We've been taught through example that people who get cancer have to endure debilitating and very expensive treatments. It sort of irks me when I hear people talk about how expensive "their cancer" treatments are. A bit of a double whammy: "their cancer" and then bragging about how much money is being spent on them.

Okay, I'm being a bit insensitive here. I know there's value in hope. Maybe there's hope that the more money is spent, the better the chances become for a cure. We all want to be seen by the best doctor. I always advocate for people who have been given this diagnosis to go see my surgeon. He is the best. I don't think that the question of how to define "the best" has been adequately studied, either. I do know I survived an unsurvivable cancer because of his care.

When I was growing up, cancer was a death sentence, but it's not so much today, with the advances in both western medicine and more knowledge and acceptance of complementary medicine.

As a brief aside, Kelly A. Turner, Ph.D. (2014) is the author of Radical Remission. She's a social worker in the field of oncology who always wondered why some people got well. In her book, she follows patients who have gone into remission and looks at some of the non-traditional approaches they pursued. It's an excellent read.

Faith healing has always fascinated me. I kind of lump faith healing and shamanistic practices into the same category; they both center around total trust and faith in the healer. Faith healing in Christianity goes back to Christ, the first person of record in the Christian religion to demonstrate the laying on of hands and healing people.

I remember in college there was a student whose family was Christian Scientist; her family didn't believe in doctors. The student became ill with scarlet fever, and the fear was that her throat would swell shut and she wouldn't be able to breathe. There was an artificial airway with our resident assistant in case this happened. Finally, the school sent that student home because they couldn't bear the burden of the liability. I never heard what happened to her. I've always wondered.

This book is not about faith healing. Several people encouraged me to pursue that course of action. I never did, but I've read about healing miracles, and I do believe it happens. I know that shamans heal the people of their tribes. My guess is that there must be incredible trust and belief that the healer can heal you and that you want to be healed.

The other thing I've noticed about faith healing is the altered state. The person being healed goes into an altered state, almost like being hypnotized. The person is very suggestible and open at that point, which could contribute to the positive results. It warrants more research, if you're interested in pursuing this avenue. I myself did not feel drawn into this area of personal healing.

In the late 1990s, I attended a lecture/debate given by Dr. Andrew Weil and the CEO of the Florida Cancer Centers. Dr. Weil supported surgically removing cancer and then working on building up your immune system to combat the disease. The CEO supported not only surgery, but also chemotherapy and radiation therapy, both of which Dr. Weil opposed. The statistics on the effectiveness of these therapies are very poor, but they're the only weapon traditional medicine has.

The two men had quite a debate about the subject. At the end, I was surprised when they found common ground by both attributing spontaneous remission to falling in love. You know, the feeling when you're all goo-goo eyed about someone and your whole world revolves around that incredible feeling of being "in love."

Several years later, a friend shared a book with me called *Miracle in Maui*, by Paul Pearsall, Ph.D. (2003), who survived a devastating cancer. He discusses manifesting miracles in your life, his premise being that you should evoke a feeling of awe frequently. Look at a sunset, a rainbow, a kitten, etc., and just feel the sensation of awe wash over you. It doesn't get any better than the feeling of awe or the feeling of being in love. These feelings are free and only have positive side effects.

I also looked into dieting and stopped eating any food with chemicals and pesticides—no soda, no hotdogs, etc. I tried a macrobiotic diet for a while, but it ultimately didn't resonate with me. As hard as I tried, I just could not stand the taste of miso.

I had been eating healthy, and my life had already been focused on doing positive things for my body, so I didn't see a lot of room for improvement in this area. If I only had a couple of years to live, I wanted to eat the foods I enjoyed; I just made sure they were made out of healthy, natural ingredients. Organic chocolate and ice cream, here I come!

But in the meantime, I had a few fun things on my bucket list. I had been told I could not go scuba diving for six months after the surgery. They wanted to make sure the dura (sac around the brain) had totally healed and sealed off, as it's not a good thing to get saltwater on the brain.

My six-month wait took me to December. I had a great relationship with a dive company in Tavernier, Florida, and I set up my dive with them.

The day finally came when I had the medical clearance to go scuba diving. I had to get CT scans every six months to look for signs of recurrence. The scan came back with no evidence of cancer, so it was time to go diving.

It was a cold, rainy, windy day in the Keys. The weather was iffy; the seas were running four to five feet. Our first scheduled dive was on the USCG Duane, a coastguard cutter scuttled off Tavernier Key as an artificial reef and dive site. The main deck was at 100 feet, the keel at about 130 feet to the sand.

I wasn't going to dive below the main deck. I'd been down on the wreck many times and was excited to have this as my first post-surgery dive.

There were five men with me on the dive boat. The divers on board were very experienced, with my own dive buddy being an instructor, so I was in good company. My greatest concern was exposing my face in front of these strong, good-looking young men. I had never exposed the surgery area in public, but I was going to have to. I couldn't wear a patch underneath my dive mask.

The dive shop owner, John Reddick, aka Capt. Redneck, had been in Special Forces in Vietnam. He was tough and ran a tight ship. His greatest concern was for my health, like what could go wrong with my brain under pressure. We had two very different concerns, but I do believe his was more important. Still, there was something to be said about wanting to know whether or not these hunks would go running off the back of the boat once I exposed my face.

We made the dive. It was rough on the surface, but great down on the cutter. We swam in and out of the superstructure, looking at corals and fish, which had really increased in the past year. I had a blast.

When we surfaced and got back on the boat, I stood there with the guys, talking about all the great things we'd seen. I was so excited and having so much fun that I forgot to be self-conscious. We moved to a shallow dive site, another of my favorites, Conch Horseshoe.

On the way back in, as we were cleaning up our gear and talking about our great day on the water, it dawned on me that no one had jumped off the back of the boat in response to my disfigured face. In fact, it turned out to have been a bit anticlimactic. No one seemed to even notice it. It was all about the camaraderie and me being able to successfully execute the dive. I was back and accepted by the dive community!

Change was also happening with my work in the adolescent treatment program. It was being slowly dismantled under managed care, even though the effectiveness of the treatment couldn't be denied. It was all about profit margin for the insurance company; the program cost too much. I found out years later that the CEO of the insurance company was making billions at the expense of people who desperately needed excellent treatment. High salaries for the administration were more important than the people they were professing to care about.

Pat, the head nurse of the adolescent unit, was a personal friend. I had dated one of her husband's co-workers who lived in the Keys. We'd go there about one weekend a month to scuba dive, fish, and water ski, our trifecta. Pat and I started talking about becoming dive masters.

Every year we took the highest-level adolescents in the program to the Keys for a week to reacclimatize them to life outside the hospital. We wanted to show them all the fun things they could do without turning to substance abuse.

Furthermore, to successfully scuba dive, you must learn to have confidence in your own skills, equipment, and those of your buddy. These were life skills these adolescents had not learned growing up. They didn't trust themselves or others. This part of the program allowed them to take the skills they had learned in the program and transfer them to everyday life.

The adolescents did a great job diving and some of them talked about trying for jobs in the dive industry. It was great to see them considering a potential positive future for themselves.

With Pat and me as dive masters, we would have the skills to assist with those dives. It was a challenging course and took our diving skills to the next level. The instructor stressed us underwater. We had to be so comfortable with the dive equipment and our personal skills that we could perform dive skills automatically so we had the freedom to help someone else. We had to learn how to fix equipment underwater to safely get a distressed diver to the surface, as well as how to give rescue breaths in the water. It was a great course.

Many years later, I realized that Pat not only did the course to help the adolescents, she did it to help me renew my own self-confidence. Mine really had gotten "all shook up" after the diagnosis.

Another friend, Jorge, a member of our Keys Trifecta group, was a merchant marine and a dive instructor. He was first mate on a tanker that sailed the Pacific Ocean, and he'd volunteered to come to West Palm Beach and teach diving to the adolescents.

Jorge told me that if I was going to be a regular in the Keys, I had to read Hemingway. So I did. Hemingway motivated me to write. He would get up early in the morning, write, and then go experience life the rest of the day. I so wanted time to experience a long life!

Jorge had a dream of becoming a harbor pilot, bringing those huge ships into port. He was studying to take a test where he had to memorize every channel, buoy, and dock in the harbor. Working hard to pursue his dreams, he was a great role model for our adolescents.

Jorge pulled me aside one day after the scuba class to make a confession. He was feeling very guilty for not having visited me in the hospital. To tell the truth, I hadn't noticed. Isn't it funny how we think things are bothering other people, when in reality they're only bothering us?

He confessed that he could not bear to be in hospitals, saying that they gave him the willies. I forgave him and expressed my appreciation for his friendship outside of the hospital.

Jorge is one of those people who keeps in touch with friends. As a Navy brat who'd always had to concentrate on making the next set of friends at my dad's new duty station, I was really bad at staying in touch. Jorge has remained a good friend throughout my life. I don't see him much, but I know he's in the world and that I can call on him if I need him. It's a nice feeling.

All people we meet have a role to play in our lives, sometimes challenging us and sometimes supporting us. A person who can't come to the hospital can still be your friend. They're just going to play a different role in your healing.

I had a connection with Dolphins Plus in Key Largo, and we set up dolphin encounters for the adolescents. It was important for us to document the effects of the encounters, so we set up a study with measurable goals.

The dolphin encounters were very successful. I remember one particular young girl who had been severely sexually abused, starting at age seven. She was now 14. Dolphins are very sexual mammals and we had taught the adolescents how to cope with unwanted interaction by just swimming to the side and getting out of the water. We were on hand to help them process their feelings.

This young woman was nudged several times by a male dolphin. She would swim away toward other dolphins in the pool. It was so interesting to me that the dolphins could almost read her fears. The females protected her, and as she gained confidence in her abilities to protect herself, she eventually made friends with the male dolphin but on her own terms. She was able to talk about how empowering this encounter had been for her, where she could set boundaries and have them respected.

The results of our study "Overcoming Fear with Trust" were published in *Dolphin Dialogue*, a journal of articles relating to dolphin therapy.

We as a staff knew this would be the last trip of this program to the Keys, as this part of the program was being shut down. I was seeing the handwriting on the wall. It was time for me to decide how I wanted to live my life, particularly given that I might only have less than a year left.

I started thinking about moving to the Keys, where I could become a dive instructor and teach diving. I could work as a therapist in the outpatient mental health center or work with the dolphins. I had options.

CHAPTER 4

Our real blessings often appear to us in the shape of pains, losses, and disappointments; let us have patience, and we shall soon see them in proper figures.

~

- Joseph Addison -

A plan was starting to form in my mind, but first, I had to follow up on a lead. A friend of a friend knew of a movie makeup company in Miami. This company made masks for monsters in horror movies. They also cast molds of famous people's faces for statues; they were incredible.

I made an appointment and was assigned to one of the best artists they had. They were going to make me an acrylic eye and a silicone eye socket that I would be able to glue into place so that with glasses, I would look like I had two eyes. People had been pushing me to look more "normal."

First, they made a mold of my orbit so the prosthesis would fit exactly. The movie company would make the socket and they sent me to sit for an artist who specialized in painting eyeballs for people with glass eyes. It looked just like my remaining eye when it was done. It was amazing.

Once the mold had been made, they poured in the liquid silicone. The prosthesis would fit perfectly into the blank space on the left side of my face. I had to pay out of pocket to have this made, as my insurance would not cover it.

The big day came when I was to have the prosthesis fitted and glued to my face. They were going to do a complete makeover. The artist didn't let me look in the mirror while she was working on me. She did my hair, poufing it up. She glued the prosthetic in place and then applied all this makeup. The makeup was heaviest along the edges of the prosthesis, so it wouldn't be noticeable.

I'm not a makeup wearer, so I was trying to figure out how I'd be able to do this. She took about two hours to get things just right. I knew that I was never going to get up two hours early to put on my eye and my makeup, except maybe for special occasions. She kept saying, "You are looking so pretty."

When it was time for the unveiling, she took me to a makeup chair turned away from the mirror. I sat in the chair and she spun me around to face the mirror.

I just stared, not recognizing the face at all. Don't get me wrong; I was beautiful, but it wasn't my face.

Tears started pouring out of the good eye. The makeup started to run. "You are so pretty," she said, and called her co-workers over to see. She thought these were tears of joy.

I couldn't talk; they were tears of grief. I tried to explain. Finally, as the tears abated, I was able to get the words out. I had been working so hard on believing I was beautiful with one eye and au natural, that when she kept saying, "you are so pretty" with my face disguised, it negated all I had worked for. To me, it was like she was saying, "you have to cover up your face to be pretty." It was so painful.

She started crying, too. It wasn't her intent to nullify my natural beauty and belief in myself; it was only her intent to do her best to follow the request to make me look "normal" again. She understood. We just hugged each other and cried.

I kept the prosthesis and tried to wear it. During the surgery, my jaw muscle had been repositioned so it was across the eye socket. Because the facial nerves had to be cut, I have very little feeling in that part of my face. Florida is hot and humid. Opening and closing my mouth, combined with the heat melting the glue, was the perfect storm, and the prosthesis would slide out of place. I wouldn't even know that it had

37

moved.

I had to be told, "Your eye is on your cheek"—a bit embarrassing when I wanted to look "normal." So, I took to wearing it only when I was going out, not eating, and going to be in a cool place. I didn't use it for daily wear, sticking instead with my patches and glasses.

I just could not find a good look. I was always changing: patch, fake eye, frosted glasses, sunglasses, etc. It was never comfortable. I did notice an interesting phenomenon. When I was uncomfortable with my looks, people around me were uncomfortable. When I was feeling comfortable and not thinking about my face, everyone else was comfortable.

It was really about my attitude. I even tested this hypothesis. I would on purpose be self-conscious or unselfconscious in a situation, and the attitude of those around me reflected my feeling. As time went on, I became more and more comfortable with my face.

Part of the issue with my face was the shrinkage of the original skin graft. My eyebrow was drifting down into my eye socket, an issue I knew I'd need to get fixed in a year or so. I was going to have to maintain my insurance in some way. Another gratitude—today I bless the Affordable Care Act.

I was not able to get insurance for cancer for many years after the operation. No insurance company wanted to cover me. When you need them, they are not there. That's why the Affordable Care Act is so meaningful to me. Insurance companies have to cover everything. I hope this rule never goes away!

With COBRA insurance, I would have six more months of coverage, so I wanted to make sure I still had it for the operation. Back then, I was not as savvy as I am now. I didn't know I'd have such trouble getting insured after letting the COBRA go. I'm so glad I waited until after the fix.

I did my one-year CT scan, ordered without contrast, but I questioned that order. All the times before, it had been done with contrast; shouldn't we be consistent? I couldn't get anyone to listen to me, though. It was cheaper to do without contrast. I went ahead and had the scan done the way they wanted.

I got a call at work; they had that number and my home number. The person calling said there were questionable results. When I was taking this call, my co-workers told me my face turned gray. I believe I stopped listening after that point. They had to do the test again with contrast. Everything came out fine the second time. Unfortunately, it cost them more in the long run to do it twice. It also cost me a week of fear that was totally unnecessary. I'm all about doing it right the first time.

I was quickly getting to the point of "to heck with insurance and work." I was not going to let cancer control my life. I wanted to go live in the Keys.

CHAPTER 5

They are ill discoverers that think there is no land, when they can see
nothing but sea.
~

- Francis Bacon -

It was just past my one-year anniversary of being cancer-free, and time to start making plans to leave my job. It was a frightening step, but I'd decided that insurance and cancer were not going to rule my life and as long as I could get my face fixed before it ran out, I was golden! My ex-boyfriend had moved out of his apartment in Key Largo, so it was for rent. I took that as a sign that it was time for me to move on. It was a small studio in the stilts of a house right on a canal, located down the street from Dolphins Plus and the Atlantic Ocean. Perfect!

I also had to sell my sailboat. I was bummed about this, but I could no longer afford it. I put it on the market and a man who was coping with lung cancer bought the boat. He planned on living on it and spending whatever time he had left in the Caribbean. It did my heart good knowing that it was going to a worthy cause.

I moved to the Keys, and let my friends know I needed work. John Reddick offered me a job, and I started working on his dive boats. I was offered a job facilitating group therapy at the local mental health clinic and had heard about a Montessori School at the Ocean Reef Club. I got a job teaching music to three- and four-year-olds and also started looking into becoming a dive instructor; they make more money than a dive master. I was following my bliss!

I had taken out my IRA, but this was not quite enough to live on with the price of the COBRA insurance. At the time I took it out, there was a 10% penalty for early withdrawal. Now, our government has decided there may be good reasons for dissolving an IRA, like health, and does not penalize people with major health problems anymore.

***

One morning, I was on my way to teach at the Ocean Reef Club when I had a remarkable spiritual experience. I had been keeping track of a friend, Jean, whose husband was fighting cancer and going through chemotherapy and radiation therapy. I am forever grateful that I didn't have to go through either of those.

As I was driving that day, I felt Jean's husband's presence. It was a palpable, warm feeling of love that washed over me. He had come to say goodbye. I pulled the car to the side of the road, but the experience was over in just a few seconds.

I found a payphone and immediately called Jean. She answered crying, saying he'd just died and she was waiting on the arrival of the children. I said, "I know. I am so sorry. He came to say goodbye."

She was stunned, and so was I. She said he'd always spoken highly of me as I'd had to go through cancer so young. Her kids came in then, so she had to get off the phone. What an incredible experience.

I know our consciousness remains after our bodies die, and for me, this encounter further validated that inner knowing. This knowing has recently turned into fact with the astounding results of the afterlife experiments being conducted at the University of Arizona by Dr. Gary E. Schwartz, Ph.D. (2002).

The other item on my agenda was to make sure I kept up with my continuing education for my therapist credentials. I had heard about a hypnosis school in nearby Miami and decided that would be a great new therapeutic skill to learn. Our instructor had worked with Dr. Brian Weiss in his landmark research on past-life regression and hypnosis. This was going to be one really interesting class. It was great, and I learned so much that I signed up to take the advanced class in wellness. The premise of this class was to access a person's beliefs regarding disease and health, modifying these beliefs to assist the person in becoming as healthy as possible.

Even though I had studied secondary gain as related to mental health, I'd never thought about it related to physical illness. In the field of mental health, some people get benefits from being ill, such as getting attention from others or controlling others by being dependent on them. In the class, I learned that there were people who just didn't want to get healthy. It reminded me of an experience I had when I went to visit my uncle in the ICU. He'd just had a heart attack, and visitors were being allowed in on a schedule for short periods of time. The ICU told me to wait in the lounge for the next visiting time.

I went into the glassed-in waiting room and it was full of smoke, which was allowed inside in those days. There was a morbidly obese woman sitting on a large couch by herself. She took up most of the couch and had her legs propped up on a couple of chairs that had been turned around. She was smoking a cigarette and there was an ashtray beside her full of butts. She had several hospital gowns all tied together to cover her.

When I walked in, she pounced. "These doctors here don't know what they're doing; they can't seem to get my heart rhythm under control." There was venom in the words as she spat them out. She gasped for breath between every few words. She put the smoked cigarette out in the ashtray, reached beside her, and picked up a large bag of potato chips. Continuing her tirade between crunches and spraying of chips, she went on to describe all the horrible, painful tests they were putting her through.

She accused the doctors of torture and said they took pleasure in sticking her and exposing her.

The doctors were not the only ones on her hit list. She then started in on the nurses and their incompetence. As she got wound up on the subject, her face began to turn red. She described the atrocities they had done to her, showing me the purple marks on her arms where the nurses had tried desperately to find a vein. It was then that I noticed an IV hanging out of her neck. It must have been the only place they could get access.

At this point, I started to feel sorry for the hospital staff. I couldn't think of anything to say in sympathy or support. I just stared and nodded. The nod launched her into a tirade about the hospital food. She talked about how they were only serving her baked fish and vegetables. They wouldn't allow her any "real" food, such as fried meat, lots of bread and butter, and dessert. She said her only choice was to sit in the waiting room and eat the food her family brought to her so she wouldn't starve to death. She offered me a store-bought chocolate roll from the bag next to her. I could only shake my head no.

All I could do was sit there and nod. I was desperately trying to think of something to say to gently get her to understand that she might have a role in the disease process, to talk to her about trying to modify her diet or quit smoking. As if she could read my mind then, she launched into another tirade, this time aimed at me. She must have seen it written all over my face that I really was not totally in agreement with her assessment of the hospital.

She accused me of not believing her. I said I was concerned for her condition and suggested she slow down her breathing and relax. She grabbed another cigarette and said, "This will slow my breathing down and relax me." I suggested she try to slow down her breathing without the cigarette.

At that moment, alarms went off as she slumped over. I saw nurses running down the hall with a gurney and a crash cart. I opened the door and made way for them to come in and help her.

There was no way they were going to get her up on the gurney. They gently slid her to the floor and opened up her gown. I watched through the glass as they initiated CPR, doing their best to bring her back to life.

I had a twinge of guilt; who was I to try to change her behavior? I could not condone what she was doing to herself, but I didn't know the whole story of how she'd ended up in this place of anger and obesity. The only comfort she had was food and cigarettes. But could I stand by and watch someone commit suicide without trying to offer assistance? It's a hard place to be, to understand.

I knew her position must have been hard as well. I knew I also had engaged in behaviors that were detrimental to my health and that doctors and nurses were not perfect. But from the little I observed, she wasn't even meeting them halfway.

Not everyone wants to be healed. Secondary gains can get in the way.

Meeting your doctors at least halfway or more is the key to health. They can't fix something while you're undoing it. I had the one treatment they could offer. It was up to me to do my best to give that treatment a chance. This hypnosis course was another step in that direction. I had to make sure I was not subconsciously doing anything to sabotage my own health. Was I getting secondary gains from having cancer? This was important for me to explore.

The first exercise in this advanced course was to explore early trauma. I learned there's a correlation between serious illness and severe trauma. Statistically, it takes about two years from a severe trauma for a serious physical illness to manifest. We all know people under stress are more susceptible to colds and flu, but I'm talking serious illnesses, like cancer, multiple sclerosis, and amyotrophic lateral sclerosis (Lou Gehrig's disease).

I started to do the math. My grandfather (the one who had lost an eyelid to skin cancer) had died two years prior to my being diagnosed with cancer. I had gone to visit a highly recommended medium after he died, hoping to learn about my past lives. Upon sitting down, she looked at me and said, "Your grandfather came in with you. He wants to talk to you. We cannot get started until he talks to you."

I was in shock, to say the least. My relationship with my grandfather had been interesting. I was the first and only girl born into the family for a couple of generations. My grandfather doted on me. Growing up, I often felt smothered by him. He was the nicest, politest, most community-conscious man alive. Everyone in the small town where he lived called him Mr. Tom. He coached generations of basketball players.

I remember that when he died, I went off the deep end; it was a totally self-destructive reaction. I had no idea why it hit me so hard. It was not the first death in the family. Most of the impact was on a subconscious level. I wanted to die to be with him. I had even done some really stupid things that could have resulted in my death. Up until now, I had not put the trauma of his death together with the cancer; were they related?

Once my grandfather had his say, he left the room. He wanted to make sure I knew he was all right. He also wanted to make sure I was all right and encouraged me to continue to live a full life. The medium went on to tell me that my grandfather and I had been together in many lifetimes. There were several in which I had been his wife and had committed suicide after his death because I didn't want to live without him. Was this the energy that had manifested as cancer this time?

I wasn't ready to die. I had chosen to live without him. Could I stop this train before it crashed? The lesson I needed to learn was to believe in myself, feel secure in myself, and not depend on others for my happiness.

It's important for someone to understand his or her deepest feelings about death in order to live freely. As such, the final exercise in this advanced course in wellness was a near-death experience. When under hypnosis, you won't do anything you don't want to do, and if it becomes too stressful, you'll spontaneously come out of the trance.

As the group—all of us under hypnosis—were led closer and closer to a near-death experience, I started to notice my heart pounding and how rapidly I was breathing. A panicked feeling came over me. I came out of trance and sat quietly while the rest of the class completed the exercise.

What was the panic attack about? I wasn't really dying; it was just an exercise, but my body reacted as if I was. I was probably the only person in the room who had been given a terminal diagnosis; maybe it was too close for comfort. I guess I was not as prepared for death as I thought.

As I have reflected back on this experience over the years, I really wonder if some of the fear and anxiety we feel around death is a survival mechanism to keep us alive. Others in the class who participated to the end talked about the wonderful, peaceful, joyful experience they had. They said they were no longer afraid of death.

Sometimes life is overwhelming and we flippantly make the remark or have a feeling, "This would be so much easier if I was dead." It's more of a feeling of "I just don't want to deal with life anymore." Maybe the anxiety I felt was my soul saying, "It's not time. Death would be simpler, but you need to stay here now." It was a very soul-searching experience for me.

I started to incorporate some of the techniques I learned from hypnosis into my therapy groups at the mental health center. I was also asked to facilitate a cancer support group. I started to really listen to the words they were saying. Were they taking possession of the cancer, always referring to it as "mine"? How did they describe the treatments they were receiving? How did they describe their prognosis? All these answers gave me insight into how the person was really coping.

I remember one man who always saw the glass as half-empty. He talked about the chemotherapy as "poison" they were putting into his body. He had no hope for the treatment. If he really believed the doctors were poisoning him, how would the chemotherapy work in his body? Would it be a self-fulfilling prophecy?

I asked him to explore his beliefs around chemotherapy and the reasons he was taking it. He said the doctors had told him it was his only chance, a last-ditch effort, one he did not believe would work. He had the hopelessness of "yes, but..." The unspoken belief was, "Yes, I will take the poison because everyone expects it of me, but it won't work."

There was another man who had been diagnosed with prostate cancer. He had had surgery and was going through radiation. He talked about the treatment with hope, about his family and wanting to live for them. He was in the group for depression; both men were. They just had such different outlooks.

You can be depressed and choose to stay there, or you can choose to get help and leave it behind. This goes back to the grooves in the record player; what we think and believe over and over again will become ingrained in our minds. Be careful with your thoughts and ingrain only those that serve you best.

So, how can any treatment work if you don't believe in it? Just look at placebo research if you want to learn how your beliefs affect the outcome of the medicines you take. People given placebos (not medicine) sometimes get well just as if they were taking the prescribed medicine. If you choose a treatment, choose it with your whole heart. Believe that it's making you better. Feel it working inside, eradicating the cancer. Help it to work!

If you decide not to take the medicine because you believe it's poison, then you're also honoring your belief system. The lesson here is to be honest with yourself and your beliefs, and do those things that are in line with those beliefs. Either that, or change your beliefs!

Maybe I was not seeing into this man's soul. I, too, have been indoctrinated by western medicine beliefs. Maybe it was time for the man who believed chemo was poison to end his journey. The medical world is all about fighting disease and preserving life. The truth is, one day we all die. Dying is hard. Those who love you don't want to let you go; you don't want to leave them. Yet it's something we all do. It is part of life, part of the journey.

Maybe the only way this man could end this stage of the journey was through contracting a fatal illness and taking "poison." Maybe he was sad and depressed because on some deep level in his consciousness he knew it was time to go. His conscious mind could not accept it. This, in the eyes of our current world belief system, is giving up.

I have always hated hearing the term "giving up." Fighting cancer takes everything you have. I know people of whom others say, "they just stopped fighting" or "they died fighting." Fighting takes so much energy that there is not much left over for enjoying life, for pursuing dreams, for living. So, the person on the final stage of their journey gets trapped. Somewhere deep in their soul, they know it's time to go. Everyone around them, friends, family, doctors, nurses, are saying *fight*. How does the person resolve this dilemma?

One way would be to take "poison," another word for chemo. Then a person can appear on the outside to be fighting the good fight, while on the inside they're following their soul. It's the cancer's fault, the treatment, the doctors let them down, etc., etc., etc.

There was a great *Northern Exposure* episode where an older woman was dying. The doctor, Joel, got her to agree to all sorts of tests so he could determine what was wrong. She was very patient with him as she tried to explain there was nothing "wrong"; it was just time for her to die. The tests all came back negative. Medically, there was nothing wrong. Yet she died.

This experience really made Joel question his ability as a doctor. It was his ego that interfered. The woman's family and friends had accepted that she was going to die and knew that there was nothing wrong; it was just time for her to transition. What an incredible place to be! To just be able to die when it's time, without having to go through illness and suffering.

"Good Lord, Joel, you're only a doctor. Do you reproach yourself when winter comes, when the grass dies, and the leaves fall from the trees? Nedra died because it was her time, and she died well. She

died with all her wits about her, with her loved ones by her side. She said all her goodbyes. You and I should only be so fortunate, Joel."

- Ruth Anne to Joel (Season 5, Episode 10).

I truly hope one day we can recognize what is right for our souls. We can get past the imposed belief that death is saying goodbye forever. We can let go of having to fight for life till death consumes us, like soldiers on the battleground. We can honor the impermanence of life and also honor death. Once we are able to do this, we can truly live and enjoy each day we have on this earth. We can "Celebrate the Journey."

CHAPTER 6

The grass is greenest right where you are.

~

- Wally "Famous" Amos -

I loved living in the Keys; it was great to spend time in nature. With such a small living space, there was very little housework to do. I was getting more involved with dolphin therapy. Our hypnosis instructor worked a lot with AIDS patients. The disease was too often fatal, and no one knew much about it at the time. Today, it has become a chronic disease, not so much a fatal one. My instructor believed that dolphin encounters might have a positive effect on people with AIDS. We discussed this with the staff at Dolphins Plus. They were open to having these patients come and experience the joy of swimming with the dolphins. The workshop was very successful, and we had several more after that first experience.

I became a dive instructor and received additional certification to instruct people with disabilities in the sport. What a great thing. Even my friend Shawn wanted to learn to dive. I remember after her first open ocean dive, I was up on the bridge of the boat, cleaning up after the trip. She was sitting on the dock, waiting for me to finish. I looked down at her and shook my head; it was just incredible for us to be there!

When we'd met in music therapy school in the Midwest, we had dreamed of tropical climes. We were so idealistic; we were going to cure the world with music. Now here we were, successful professionals, making a positive difference in the lives of our patients and spending our fun time hanging out in the Keys. Who would have believed it? Okay, so she was in a wheelchair due to a paralyzing virus, and I was coping with cancer, but we were living the life. So much to be grateful for!

The pace of my life was slower than it had been for years. There was time to reflect, time to work at jobs I loved, and time to enjoy the natural world. I was meditating daily, getting lots of exercise, spending time with friends, and growing professionally. Then it happened, an experience that has stayed with me my whole life, and one I rarely talk about, because no one would believe me.

I did recently share it with a friend who was diagnosed with ACC. Her husband was there, and he makes a study of religious texts. He said that the Apostle Paul described a similar experience, so maybe my experience is not so unusual. I would love to know if others also have had this experience. I cannot believe I am alone. Believe me, there is nothing that special or pious about me.

I was just finishing up cleaning my apartment when I heard a voice. The voice was male and quiet, but firm. It came from both inside and outside my head.

"Do you want to live or die?" The question was asked in the same casual tone as someone would say, "Do you want chocolate or vanilla ice cream?"

I knew I had to make the decision right then. I got an impression that to die would mean a short period of discomfort and then an incredible way of being—joyful, peaceful, and wonderful. It was very enticing. The impression of living was more challenging. Whichever way I went would be fine. There was no right or wrong. Just like ice cream is ice cream, it was just your choice of flavor.

I didn't hesitate. Always up for a challenge, I chose life. From that moment on, I knew cancer would not cause my demise. I would live much longer than two years. I finished cleaning house and got ready for my next job.

I fell into a rhythm in the Keys, teaching, playing, and relaxing. I enjoyed the relaxed lifestyle and got the Keys disease. I could feel myself becoming more and more apathetic, losing my fighting edge. It can be a very insidious sickness, and alcohol is a big part of the picture. Alcohol and I have had our ups and downs, and I wasn't sure which direction I was headed.

I had friends from Clearwater who were racing sailboats down to Key West, and they invited me to join them in Key West for the party. The Clearwater Key West Race at the time was "the sailboat regatta of the year." It's also the party of the year! One of the big rum distilleries always sponsors the race.

I headed down to the party and met up with sailing buddies. We enjoyed the rum, the sun, the music, and dancing. One of my friends started talking to me about moving back to Clearwater. It was tempting. I was still on my COBRA insurance and not sure what I was going to do when it ran out. I did not have a full-time job and knew no one was going to insure me with cancer.

I had learned to sail big boats offshore when I lived in Clearwater in 1985. I had been involved with a club called Windjammers and became a regular racing crewmember on a C&C 38 named *Polyphonic*, owned by Jeff Grossman, a fabulous teacher and racer. Jeff and his wife currently own the "Two Can Sail" company. My first lesson was learning to be rail meat, meaning that I moved my body weight around the boat so that the boat was positioned optimally in the water for the most speed. I just followed the orders of the captain and went where he wanted me to seat my meat.

The next position I learned was grinding, where I stood over a winch and turned it like crazy to trim the sails. The sails are the engine of the boat, and must be trimmed just right in coordination with the helm (steering) to get optimal speed. The trimmer told you when to start and stop. This took lots of upper body strength, so my windsurfing days definitely benefited me in this area.

I eventually graduated in position to trimmer, so I could tell my grinder what to do. I loved trimming sails! I also did a few stints on foredeck. The foredeck is responsible for raising and lowering the sails. If there's a race with lots of wind changes and distance, the foredeck is kept very busy. The foredeck is small and dangerous. The captain wants the lightest and strongest crewmembers up there; it's a very demanding job. My lack of depth perception was not an asset on the foredeck!

After a particularly grueling race, a wonderful friend of mine, and great foredeck crewmember, Judy, said, "The sails were going up and down faster than a whore's drawers!"

Eventually, I was allowed to helm in the women's races and some of the long-distance races. Jeff had also started teaching me about offshore and racing navigation, weather, wind, and currents. There's so much to learn in sailing, I never get bored. It's a really complex sport with lots of moving parts. Regarding moving parts, it can be very dangerous. There are very high-tension loads on the lines and spars. I remember a race where our main mast came down. It was scary, but we were well-trained, no one was hurt, and we got the boat back to the dock safely.

Yes, I still had some wonderful connections in Clearwater. One of Jeff's crew was looking for a roommate. These coincidences made me feel like I was being led down another path, so I started making preparations to head to back to Clearwater. This area would have good job prospects and lots of opportunities for sailing. The jobs I'd pieced together in the Keys were not really enough to live on.

The Keys are expensive. I was supplementing my income with my IRA. It wouldn't last forever. I knew I would outlive it!

I also was coming up on two years cancer-free. I wanted to get settled before I had the next operation to make my face look more normal. The Montessori school was getting out for the summer, so this would be a good time to make the move. I gave my notice and made preparations, staying on part-time at the dive center as I was still teaching classes and could travel back to the Keys to finish those commitments.

I got settled in my new home. There was plenty of room for my two cats and me, as long as they did not meet my roommate's bird face to face. Speaking of faces, it was time to get my face fixed.

I made the appointment with Dr. Wolfe and made arrangements to stay with Shawn in Miami. She would transport me to the hospital. The surgery was only going to take a few hours; no overnight stay this time. I arrived at Shawn's house the night before the operation and had a restless night, scared that they would find more cancer when they opened me up. Even though I had a belief that all was well, there were still nagging doubts. Those little nagging doubts can get the best of you at times.

I woke the next morning, determined to put my wishes in writing before I went under the knife. I wrote up a paper that said if they found any cancer, they were to just close the wound and wake me up. I didn't want to wake up with even more of my face missing. I also put in writing that if there *was* cancer, I wanted to discuss the next steps with the surgeon and a counselor. I signed it and had Shawn and her roommate, Beth, sign it as witnesses. This was in the days before living wills were the norm.

I actually drove myself to the hospital, as I did not have to be there as early as Shawn had to go to work. The plan was for her to pick me up that evening and then drop me back to get my car the following morning, for the surgical follow-up. I went into pre-op and gave them my paper. The nurse asked if this was legal. I said yes, these were my wishes for my body and they better be honored.

Off I went to surgery. As I was coming out of the anesthesia, I heard the nursing talking about not being able to keep a patient's blood pressure up. They called the doctor for adrenalin to rouse the patient. I was at the point of hearing what was going on, but I couldn't talk yet. As I roused more, I opened my eye, and expressed sympathy for what was going on with the other patient.

The nurse looked at me like she was seeing a ghost. She said, "It's *your* blood pressure we can't get up."

"Oh," I replied. "You know I haven't eaten since last night; maybe some juice or something will get things right."

The nurse brought me some juice. I then looked at her and said, "Is the cuff on correctly?"

She said, "The anesthesiologist put it on in surgery; I'm sure it's fine," as she gave me another dose of adrenaline.

The nurse added, "They only did what you asked them to do. You will feel a lot of bandages, but everything is fine."

At that point, another nurse walked by and looked down at my arm, then looked at the nurse tending me and said, "Do you know this blood pressure cuff is on upside down?"

They reapplied the cuff correctly and now my blood pressure was higher than normal and I was feeling very spunky. The doctor came in and told me that there had been no sign of cancer and that the graft was a success. I was so relieved! Even though I knew in my heart the doctor wouldn't find any cancer, it was sure nice to have it validated. He said that as soon as I ate something and went to the bathroom, I could go home, as long as I had a driver. I told him a friend was coming by after work to pick me up.

They took me up to a room where I ate my dinner and used the bathroom, leaving the evidence in the toilet. I was still feeling very spunky, or maybe I should say irritable and anxious, due to all the extra adrenaline running around in my system, and was very ready to put the hospital behind me.

The nurse said I had to wait until she'd had her dinner, and I was not pleased about that. A patient shot full of adrenaline is not very patient! Shawn came in and that made me even more anxious to get out of there. Shawn has this wicked sense of humor.

She said, "When the nurse comes in, she better ask, 'Will the real patient please stand up?'" I just cracked up. Shawn was referring to the original surgery when they'd tried to keep her and send me home.

Eventually, the nurse came in and I got my walking papers. As we made our way to the parking garage, I told Shawn that I didn't want to get up as early as she had to the next morning, and it made more sense for me to drive myself back to her house so I would have my car. I was able to convince her of that plan, but then realized I didn't have much gas so we'd need to stop at a gas station.

We pulled into a gas station a couple of blocks from the hospital in an area of Miami known as "Little Havana." I jumped out of the car, still running on adrenaline, and started pumping my gas. I was standing there in my white turban of bandages covering up the area of my left eye. You should have seen the looks I was getting.

All gassed up, we drove back to Shawn's for a nice, quiet evening and celebration that I was still cancer-free.

***

After my surgery, it was back to Clearwater and job hunting. Also, I had to schedule some time in the Keys to finish up dive lessons. I set up the lessons for August and updated my résumé. About this time, my dad called to tell me that my grandmother was really sick and that he was driving to Kentucky to bring her to their home in Melrose, Florida. I put the job search on hold and made arrangements to go and assist.

My grandmother was bedbound, and she was admitted to the hospice home care program. We were so pleased to be able to have her with us, and she was pleased to be surrounded by family. She died peacefully a couple of weeks later.

I rescheduled the open water dives with my students for the end of August in Key Largo. Just as I was getting my stuff together, South Florida had an unwelcome visitor, Hurricane Andrew. It was several weeks after Andrew went through before we were able to drive down US-1 to the Keys. I have never been through a war zone, but Homestead looked like pictures of bombed-out cities that I'd seen on the news.

It was surreal. National Guardsmen lined the streets with automatic weapons to prevent looters. There were pieces of rope driven through palm trees and I couldn't figure out my favorite shortcut, as all the landmarks were gone.

My friend's worksite, a fish farm, was on the old Aerojet property, where NASA had tested rocket fuel in the Everglades. My friend showed me where they had spent the storm. They had taken shelter in one of the old Aerojet bunkers. The bunker was made to withstand blasts from missiles and rockets. He said the thick steel doors of the bunker had been flexing, and they'd put tons of fish food against the doors to prevent them from opening. He said the sound was terrifying, like if you were sitting under a freight train! Outside the bunker, there was a one-inch thick steel table with an I-beam driven through it by the wind. The power of this storm blew my mind.

As I headed south to Key Largo, there was a demarcation line. The trees were non-existent leaving Homestead, and about halfway down the highway, the trees started again. It looked like a huge lawnmower had just cut a swath across the foot of Florida. I have tremendous respect for Mother Nature. As much as man has tried to make nature conform to his wishes, it is futile. Better to work with the natural forces instead of against.

The diving classes in Key Largo went well, and then it was back to Clearwater. My dad called to tell me that my grandmother had left me a little money. I was getting hooked up with some dive shops in

Clearwater, so I decided to use the money to take a dive vacation to Roatán, Honduras. Shawn also wanted to go, so we both signed up.

The trip was incredible. The resort was far off the beaten path, so we could only get there by boat. There was beach diving and boat diving. The proprietors built ramps for Shawn in anticipation of her coming, to make the resort accessible. The dive master and captain took care of all of Shawn's transport and equipment needs. We had a great time.

CHAPTER 7

There are many points on the compass rose. I had to locate the few
that were meant for me and head for this that summoned me with a
passion, for they were the ones that gave meaning to my life.

~

- Richard Bode -

Finally, it was time for a real job, with insurance. A full-time
employer would provide health insurance for me for everything but
cancer. Welcome back to the real world!

My new job was at a treatment facility for adolescents. It was a good
program. We had a ropes course and I became a ropes facilitator. What
a wonderful experience for the adolescents! They learned how to
cooperate, trust, and depend on each other. Putting your words into
action is really the key. You can talk about the changes you're going to
make all day, but putting the words into action and feeling the
consequences of those actions makes the difference.

Unfortunately, after I'd worked there for about two years, the facility
was sold and the therapists were laid off. I finally found another job at a
county-run facility for adolescents.

At this time, I was still struggling with feeling unattractive and with
how to present my face to the public. One of my patients was a 13-year-
old boy diagnosed with schizophrenia, who had been terribly abused
and neglected. He taught me not to be ashamed of my scars, and set me
straight on how to cope with my face issue.

One day during a session, he asked me why I always covered up the side of my face with the scar. I could not think of a good answer, so like a good therapist, I turned the question around on him.

He said to me, "You have taught me not to be ashamed of my scars, even though they're invisible. Are you ashamed of your scar?"

"No, I'm not," I replied. "There is no reason to be ashamed of something I had no control over." But my mind went racing to why I was always trying to cover up my face, making it look normal. I would never look like I did before cancer.

This young man would never have the innocence he was born with. We could both release our shame and go confidently into the world.

"Well then, I won't be ashamed of being abused. I had no control over what those people did to me," he replied. He had a really strong inner core that he attributed to the Boy Scouts. His experiences with them had given him an internal resource he could draw on to succeed, despite the horrible abuse he had suffered.

"Well, I will stop covering up my scar and hold my head high," I decided. We shook on it!

From that day on, I continued to wear glasses for protection, and on special occasions, I would wear a fancy patch. Most of the time, though, it was take me or leave me, but don't judge me for how my face looks. Out of the mouth of babes—sometimes children have such incredible wisdom.

***

Finally, five years had gone by and it was time for my final scan. The doctor told me that if I remained cancer-free for five years, I was clear. I anxiously awaited the call from the radiologist to let me know if there was evidence of cancer. When he called and let me know there was no evidence of cancer, I jumped for joy. I started planning my "I made it" party! It was time to celebrate and get a life! I threw a huge party. Friends from music therapy school in Kansas City came, along with friends who had worked in the program in West Palm Beach, and of course, all of my sailing buddies. There were close to 100 people at the party. We played volleyball until dark, then celebrated well into the night. It was a blast.

* * *

Sailing continued to be a focus in my life. I continued to learn about sailing big boats offshore. A friend was putting together an all-women's team to race from St. Petersburg Yacht Club in St. Petersburg, Florida to Isla Mujeres, Mexico, an island off the coast of Cancun on the Yucatan Peninsula. This race, the Regatta del Sol al Sol, happens every year.

There had never been an all-women's team in the race. The skipper, a local sail maker named Linda, borrowed a 40-foot wooden boat from her friend, Mike. Mike had built the boat in South Africa and sailed it to the United States. The hull was solid cold-molded mahogany, and the keel was made from reclaimed lead pipes.

There were eight of us selected for the crew. Most of us were small boat racers; very few had done extensive offshore sailing. We were all tough and game. We helped get the boat and engine ready for the trip, including helping Linda make the sails. Our main sponsor was Juice Plus, so our spinnaker was orange and white with their logo on it. Our t-shirts and shorts also said "Juice Plus."

We had many other sponsors who donated paint, equipment, emergency supplies, etc., to the trip.

Each team member chose a specialty. I chose navigation since I had always been very interested in navigation and weather. Noel, a former crewmate on a multi-hull on which I raced, offered to teach me about offshore navigation. Noel was a former Navy pilot who knew his stuff. He taught me to use the LORAN and a sextant in case we lost all of our power. We also had a newfangled instrument called the Global Positioning System (GPS). This was a satellite system and was touted to be more accurate than LORAN. We had a GPS on board as backup, but I didn't know much about its accuracy.

LORAN, which uses waves from radio towers on land to give you coordinates, was still the tried and true navigational tool. LORAN numbers are different from the latitude and longitude numbers on the chart, so the chart had to have both. However, both GPS and LORAN depended upon electricity, and the only power generator on the boat was the engine. If we lost the engine, we couldn't use the LORAN or GPS. Since we would be offshore, out of sight of land, Noel taught me to dead reckon and use a sextant for noon sights.

Dead reckoning is a guesstimate of where you are based on time, speed, and compass heading. I learned how to drop a chip of wood off the bow and count the seconds to when it reached the stern to get our speed through the water, another skill to use in case of power loss. So, at every hour, I would get our speed, time, and compass heading. I would then mark that place on the chart, compensating for current and drift.

At noon, I would pull out the sextant and take several shots of the sun as it reached its zenith and started back down. Using this, nautical declination tables, and math, I could determine our longitude. I became accurate within 30 nautical miles. This was considered good! I kept a running log of LORAN, sun sites, and dead reckoning. These three tools allowed me to have a good idea of where we were on the water. They validated each other.

We broke the crew up into two groups of four. Linda was in charge of one group, and I was in charge of the other. Each group did shifts of four hours on, four hours off. The race started in nasty weather; a cold front had come down from Canada and there was rain and heavy wind. We were not first off the starting line, but with about four days and 555 miles to go, we were more concerned with safety than speed.

We watched the leaders in the fleet leaving the bay, coming out of the protection of Egmont Key into the open gulf. One of the biggest boats was under full spinnaker; I could see the strain on that big, colorful sail ballooning out in front of their boat. Suddenly, the boat rolled over on its side, a broach! Then *bam*, I heard the boom, a pole that supports the bottom of the main sail in the boat, break as it hit the water. I could see the crew running around frantically to get the boat back upright and the sails out of the water. It did not appear that anyone was hurt. Now they had to turn around and go back into port for repairs, not a good way to start a race.

We looked at each other on *Hexe* and thought, *if this full crew of strong men lost control of their spinnaker and boat, the wind must be honkin'!* "Down with the spinnaker," Linda called, and we set up a smaller sail plan so as not to break our boat before we even got started!

As an all-woman crew, we were able to joke and pull pranks on each other. Patty was our number one prankster. I was very paranoid about commercial boat traffic, especially at night. Tugboats could be hundreds of feet from the barges they were towing up the coast. If you tried to sail between the tug and the tow, your boat could be cut in half by the cable connecting them. Then there were the shrimp boats with their huge nets deployed—you sure didn't want to get too close to them.

A sailboat's average speed is about the walking speed of a person on land, three to five miles per hour, sometimes a little faster; eight to ten miles per hour in the right conditions. A freighter, on the other hand, moves along at over 25 miles an hour. They are coming at you faster than you believe, and you can't get out of their way very easily. At night, each ship and boat must carry lights, which will tell you the type of vessel and whether it has a tow.

Ships don't have brakes and are not very maneuverable. The freighters, commercial fishing boats, shrimp boats, and tug and tows have right of way. They are also much bigger than you are and you would not win that collision! This falls under the "bigger boat rule!" You must know where the shipping lanes are and make sure you take evasive action early. I was always asking the crew if they saw any lights or boats. I wanted to make sure they were always watching.

Early one morning, as Patty (on my shift) was coming off watch and the next crew was coming on duty, Linda asked if they had seen any other boats. The general answer was no. As Patty got to the bottom of the steps, she turned, looked up into the cockpit, and said, "Not if you don't count the sailboat with a crew of naked men."

"What!!!" Linda's crew yelled. "Why didn't you wake us?" "There were only four of them," she replied, and made her way to the head to wash her face and get ready for bed.

We had a great laugh below as we listened to them discussing this revelation, trying to determine if she was being truthful or not! It kept them busy all shift.

Debbie was first on the helm of the other shift. She had raced dinghies (small sailboats) for years and could really drive a boat. When she was driving, the boat moved through the water like silk. All of us tried to get some sleep when Debbie was at the helm! The truth of what I had once been told became obvious—to really learn to sail, learn to sail a dinghy first! I had been crewing for dinghy sailors, but I had not had the opportunity to drive. Driving is fun, and the owner of the boat does not want to relinquish the helm!

As navigator, I had couple of chores that needed to be done hourly.

First I took our position from the LORAN and charted it. I also took our heading, speed, and time, and marked this on the chart. Ideally, they should come out in the same place. My crewmate Sharla (on the other shift) assisted me when I was resting.

The other hourly chore was tapping the barometer and writing down the reading, which would give us the weather. If the barometer was falling, we were in for a storm; if it was steady or going up, we were in for fair weather. It was a crude tool, but we found it very helpful. The weatherman was calling for easterly breezes of 15 knots as we got closer to the Caribbean. But our barometer kept rising, telling us fair weather and no wind.

As we got close to Isla Mujeres, the wind died. Our barometer was correct for the small piece of water we were sitting upon. We sat in the Gulf Stream off Cuba and sat and sat, the sails slapping, as we drifted slowly toward Cuba. The Atlantic looked like a millpond.

Swim call! We dangled a line over the side of the boat and rigged the vang, a pulley system that is attached to the boom and holds down the main sail, as a woman lift. We then took turns jumping in and swimming, as we now had a way to get back up on the boat. It gets hot in the Caribbean!

We spent so much time becalmed; we were going to have to make a decision. Were we going to forfeit the race, start the engine and engage the prop, or were we going to sail in? We still had many miles to go. We kept watching the barometer and it was holding steady; there was no change, which indicated no wind! Finally the decision was made for us, some of the crewmembers had planes to catch, and we had to get into port. As the wind was making no effort to help, we started the engine and put it in drive.

We made our approach at night. Not my first choice, but that was where we were. Sharla and I had been faithfully marking the chart hourly and not getting much sleep. I started seeing flashing lights on the horizon and I knew there was a dangerous reef located along the coast. My chart dead reckoning said we were seven miles from the reef. The LORAN told me we were getting really close to the reef. What was right? I was exhausted and my brain felt muddled.

Sharla asked if she could help. I took a GPS reading and it said we were seven miles from the reef, just where the dead reckoning put us.

We started talking it over. What was really throwing me off was the blinking red lights. They looked so near. Were we really close to the reef? Were we in danger of running aground? We could turn around and sail offshore and wait until morning; that would be the safe thing to do.

Sharla suggested trying to contact the race committee at Isla Mujeres. The race committee was a Mexican Navy vessel stationed in the main channel. I got on the radio and called, "Club de Yates (pronounced it *yates* like *gates*, with my slight southern twang), Club to Yates, Club de Yates. This is the vessel *Hexe*, come in, please."

They replied, "We read you vessel *Hexe*; this is Club de Yates" (pronounced yacht-tes). Oops, I had already massacred the language; they knew an American was calling! They suggested firing a flare off the bow of their ship and we would see it, then they would fire a second flare, so we could get a compass bearing. That sounded like a great idea. I went up to the bow of *Hexe* and waited on the first flare, with my bearing compass in hand. Bingo. First flare was dead ahead, and so was the second. The LORAN was wrong; my dead reckoning and GPS were correct. We headed into port.

The yacht club sent a small launch out to meet us and lead us to the dock. Once tied up, customs came aboard to check our passports and deliver beer and tequila! That's what I call hospitality. We celebrated, then I went forward on the boat to the bow and rolled up in the jib sail, which was lying on the foredeck, and went to sleep!

We had such a wonderful reception in Isla Mujeres, the women's crew on the Island of Women. We were given traditional embroidered dresses and invited to participate in a maypole-type ceremony. We were given gifts and accolades wherever we went. What an incredible experience.

I've since learned that the curvature of the earth made the flashing red lights on the towers at the airport in Cancun look like they were at water level. I also learned that the LORAN towers in this part of the world are few and far between, so LORAN is not as accurate as GPS. It also really helped me solidify my skills as an offshore sailor and navigator.

***

When I returned to Clearwater, Jeff Grossman asked me to do the Clearwater Key West race on his boat, *Polyphonic*. Off I went again, in less than a week. Good thing I had lots of vacation time at that point! We were sailing across Florida Bay when the weather got ugly. Florida Bay is a very shallow body of water that can chop up quickly. The sailing term "beating" takes on a whole new meaning; we were taking a beating as the boat pounded through the chop. *Polyphonic* was a strong boat, and we knew she could take it.

Darkness fell, and the excitement began. Why do emergencies always seem to happen at night? We noticed other boats in the race stopping and changing sails. We were having the same discussion on *Polyphonic*. The wind was just at the edge of being able to carry our big "number one" jib, when we sailed into an area of total darkness and low visibility. It was like someone turned off all the stars and the lights of the boats around us.

Suddenly, a cold blast of air came directly down from the heavens and spun us in a circle, then nothing. It became quiet. We were grabbing for lines and pulling down the "number one" as it had shredded in the down draft. As we were getting ready to put up the smaller number two, a repeat of the downdraft happened, spun us the other way, and spit us out into 25-knot winds.

It turned out we had been in a waterspout and were unable to see it in the dark. We had no time to be afraid, only to react and do what we needed to take care of the boat.

I was learning a lot about sailing offshore, in weather, and with a crew. These lessons would stand me in good stead for the future. I participated in several more Key West races over the years and even got to go on a cruise after one of the races to the Dry Tortugas and gunkhole up the west coast of Florida.

***

I was getting a lot of experience in crewing, but not much at the helm. I crewed for a gentleman named Peter on a Coronado 15, a 15-foot sailing dinghy. Peter was an incredible helmsman and I loved to crew on the Coronado 15; it has a trapeze and as crew, I got to fly out over the water. It was so exhilarating.

Peter and I did very well as a team for the couple of years I crewed for him. He would not let me helm though, unless it was a women's race. I figured if I was going to really learn to drive a boat, I would need to buy my own racing dinghy. I was not competitive anymore with windsurfing because of my vision, but with a crew to be my eyes, I could get back into racing as the skipper!

I bought my own Coronado 15 and fixed it up. My friend Mike Taylor helped and crewed for me. He was such a good sport. I tea bagged him on many occasions. This is when you dip the person hanging out on the trapeze in the water. And I flipped the boat upside down so many times, they threatened to put the boat's name, along with my name and telephone number, on the bottom. But I finally learned and was able to keep the boat more right-side up than upside down.

There is a yearly women's race in the Tampa Bay area and it was getting close to that time again. I was excited to compete in my own boat, but I needed a female crew. I met a woman named Jacquie Albina, originally from the Bahamas. She owned a Hobie 18 and was open to crewing for me, if I would crew for her. Her only stipulation was that she did not swim. Not that she could not swim; she DID NOT swim! This meant I would have to sail more conservatively and keep the boat upright. It sailed faster upright, anyway.

We not only won everything in the women's races, we beat the men in the regular season. She was awesome at calling tactics on the course and I just had to steer straight, keep the boat upright, and not hit anything!

CHAPTER 8

Certainly every man that goes to sea in a little boat learns terror and salvation, happy living, air, danger, exultation, glory and repose at the end; and they are not words to him but realities which will afterwards throughout his life give the mere words a full meaning.

~

- Hilaire Belloc -

A good friend of mine, Susan (a recreational therapist), and I had a dream of making sailing accessible to people with disabilities. Sailing had become my refuge, a place of healing. I had benefited from the sport of sailing in so many ways, I wanted to share it with others. It was a chance to give back and share the sport that was such an integral part of my healing experience.

I learned about a program called the Sailing Program for People with Disabilities (SPPD). This program provided sailing opportunities to people with disabilities who were in the community and in rehabilitation, along with training sailors who wanted to compete in the Paralympics. I volunteered with SPPD, helped rig boats and helped get people in and out of boats, and was eventually asked to crew.

The focus was on Paralympic elite sailors and racing, not on community sailing. "Community sailing" is the term we used to provide people with disabilities a chance to get out on water and learn a new skill. A group of volunteers put together the community side of the program. It was our belief that people with disabilities needed the opportunity to learn to sail and captain their own boats. Where were the Paralympians (elite sailors) going to come from? They had to start somewhere. Most of the elite sailors I met had started in community programs, some before their injury and some afterward. This was the only venue in Tampa Bay where it was accessible!

I loved the challenge of making the boats accessible. Each person with a disability has his or her own individual needs. It is not a "one size fits all" situation. The person with the disability has a limited ability to adapt; the boat must instead be adapted to the person. We worked together to make sure each person had what they needed to sail independently.

The part of the sailing program for the community and rehabilitation used a little boat called a Bauer 12. The members of SPPD started to talk about a project where they'd have someone sail the Bauer 12 from St. Petersburg, Florida, to Camden, Maine. They had picked the sailor and were getting things in place. I just heard about it on the fringes and was getting more and more involved in the community program. It was so much fun, and it was challenging.

I had once again changed jobs and now was working for Suncoast Hospice. I felt like I had found a home; I loved my job as a hospice counselor. It was such rewarding work helping people to live fully until the day they died. Once again, I was told I could have health insurance for all other issues, but not for cancer. But now that I was cancer-free, I was not as concerned.

But the wind never blows in one direction; for me the wind is constantly changing and challenging me. One day, a SPPD board member, Ken, pulled me aside and asked me if I would sail the Bauer 12 to Camden, Maine. I was shocked. I told him I needed to think about it and talk to my boss about taking a three-month leave of absence. Work agreed, and I was able to COBRA my insurance once all my holiday and sick time ran out.

I called Ken and told him I'd be able to do it. He said, "You may hate me for this." I didn't understand what he meant, and he didn't elaborate. Why would I hate him for this wonderful opportunity to work with expert sailors, learn new skills, push my abilities, and promote the mission? I would be letting people know that having a disability shouldn't keep you from pursuing your dreams. It was a win/win all the way around.

The purpose of the trip was to spread the word that people who have suffered significant life traumas can still live their life's dreams and passions. After all, the Americans with Disabilities Act's motto is *"to boldly go where everyone else has gone before."*

People with disabilities have unique knowledge, drive, and experience gained through overcoming obstacles, both physical and mental. Ideas are born from our partnering with people with disabilities and understanding the strong contribution they make to our community. That experience shared can improve all of our lives.

Donations to the sail went toward furthering the success of disabled sailing programs for youths and adults, providing accessible boats, sailing lessons, and funding to Paralympic teams, as well as providing training and technology to level the field of sailing so anyone can leave their disability on the dock.

Chris Bauer, owner of Bauteck Marine in St. Augustine, Florida, builds the Bauer 12, a very pretty little boat with classic lines. He builds them primarily to be used as tenders for larger boats. Chris was modifying one to be used for the trip.

I met with several of the board members of SPPD. We set a date for launch and started a list of to-dos. The plan was for me to sail the boat from St. Petersburg with newspaper and TV coverage, parties, and fundraisers all the way to Maine.

SPPD had originally asked another sailor to do the trip, but Ken told me that not only was he not a good enough sailor, but he'd been asking for a lot of money and was giving ultimatums regarding the trip. I didn't know this other skipper very well, but did know that he had successfully done the same trip in a sea kayak. In fact, I had had a conversation with him and he'd talked about how wonderful the Bauer 12 was and that he would even sail it across the Gulf Stream to the Bahamas. The confidence he had in the boat was reassuring.

Personally, I had felt for a long time that I needed to minimize and simplify things in my life. I immediately started making a list of all of the gear that I thought I needed for the trip. It grew to be quite a large list; so much for minimizing! I only had a small boat and I needed to decide what was necessary for my survival and for the mission; a wonderful exercise in simplicity. I set up a practice schedule and set to work on building a support team and finding sponsors.

I believed I was supposed to do something important with my life, something out of the ordinary, and I loved the idea of an adventure for a worthy cause. I have always been very good at promoting things for others, and this was a great opportunity to really help make others' dreams come true. All my life experiences had been leading up to this trip. What an incredible way to bring things together: my work as a therapist, my abilities as a sailor, and my own survival of a rare cancer.

I had a friend, a Paralympic sailor, whom I admired for what he had done with his life—going from the despair of finding himself paralyzed from the chest down, to losing his business and not being able to do all the things he loved, to coming back, living life fully, and becoming a champion.

I, too, wanted to make my mark. This trip was not about me, though; it was about helping others, which was the only way I could justify spending the money and time to make it happen. I would also give over 100% to make sure that it happened and take bare minimal reimbursement for myself, because it was not about me. It was about people who needed a chance in life to know they did not need to be limited by their disability. I was totally caught up in the romance of the trip.

I scheduled speaking engagements in the community, looking not only for financial support for the trip and the program, but also for equipment. It was at Sail Expo St. Pete in November of 1999 that we had our first break in major sponsorship. Lewmar (a company that makes winches for boats) had already donated $5,000 to the trip. Dutchman (a company that makes reefing systems for boats) donated the reefing system, and JSI (Johnson Sails Inc.), a sail-making company in St. Petersburg, made a tent to cover the boat for sleeping at night. But there was so much more that was needed: money for expenses, an outboard engine for emergencies, GPS, VHF radio, charts, safety equipment, etc.

My friend Jennifer was part owner of a sail making business and she had a booth right across from *Sail Magazine* at Sail Expo. She told Tom Casey, Southeast Advertising Director of *Sail Magazine*, about the intended trip. He wanted to meet me, so Jennifer got us together.

Tom became my champion. He was intrigued by the idea and loved the mission. He set up a sponsor-seeking trip at the Miami boat show for February. I needed to shove off in April due to weather conditions and time. I was pushing it, but I knew that it would come together.

On my days off from work, I would meet with board members to plan and organize for the trip and sail the boat. We set up the first overnight on the boat for Thanksgiving weekend. I brought all my gear, with plenty of warm clothes as a cold front was expected.

A couple from the board were going to take out their larger cruising boat and we were going to sail together to an anchorage and make a long weekend of it. But there were several things that came up, including a nasty cold front, and we never made the trip. Instead, we spent most of the time making our equipment wish list, planning promotional ideas, taking pictures, and making a brochure.

Ken gave me some charts, and I started working on an itinerary. I wasn't sure how far I could go each day, as I had never tested the boat for speed and distance; I just estimated the best I could. Ken was putting pressure on me to let them know the itinerary so that they could start making arrangements in the ports that I would be visiting.

We enlisted the help of a young woman studying public relations, and she started making lists of contacts in the major cities that I would visit along the coast. I needed to stay close to the coast to get the most out of the publicity. We discussed a name for the boat over lunch. It seemed like hours of throwing out names before Ken finally said the word "prevail," and *Prevail* it was.

It was finally time for the Miami Boat Show. I towed the boat down to Miami early and we set it up in the Bauteck Marine booth with the tent erected. As we were putting the finishing touches on the boat, a Honda representative came by with several outboard engines and put one on the back of the boat. He said for us to take it; he had to give away so many at the show, anyway. We thanked him and went off to seek sponsors.

First stop was the Nissan booth for an interview with *Soundings Magazine* and to discuss which outboard motor would work best. I was wearing my uniform, my Sailing Angels shorts, donated to the trip, and my *Prevail* shirt. Photos were taken with the 3.5 horsepower engine, and we made arrangements to take delivery on it after the show.

Now, I had two outboard engines. Having a backup engine is always a good idea. After that, it was off to Magellan to talk about a GPS. They had an incredible state-of-the-art handheld machine with a chart pack. I could insert a computer chip and see myself sailing along on the chart on the screen. We'd take it!

More photos, and off to C-MAP to get the charts donated for the GPS. They gave them to us on loan. Actually, they loaned us two sets, because before all was said and done, SIMRAD donated a mounted GPS with chart pack capability, a mounted VHF radio, handheld VHF radio, and an autopilot to the cause. They also did a publicity spot at their booth as part of a cocktail party for their major clients in the industry.

Then it was off to ACR Electronics, Inc. for safety equipment. They outdid themselves, providing an EPIRB (Emergency Positioning Indicating Radio Beacon) in case I got lost at sea, all sorts of lights, flares, and a large floating bag to put it all in. They were so nice, I don't think I stopped smiling all day. I felt like a princess.

The generosity of the marine industry was overwhelming. I must have been on the right path, because everything was falling into place. Whatever we asked for was given to us for the trip. West Marine donated all the necessary little items that were needed in between, such as a life jacket, a cup, lines, hardware, and much more! This was going to be the most technologically advanced 12-foot boat anywhere.

I needed something to charge all this equipment on board, and a solar panel connected to a bank of batteries was the answer. I was given a solar panel for the trip and the batteries to store the electricity to be used as needed. For good measure, a radar reflector was thrown in to make me visible to larger ships.

Gill provided foul weather gear for both the warm waters of the south and the cold ones of the north. Tilley sent me a hat that would fit my head correctly. Mr. Carl Tilley had given me the one right off of his head at the Mobility Cup in Toronto, Ontario, Canada the year before. I was excited about having one that fit me properly. It is a great hat!

I left the boat show on a high, ready for anything. The next step was to do an overnighter. I had yet to take the boat offshore or overnight, and we had not tested the boat to see if I could right it if it capsized or if it would sink. It was less than six weeks to the start of the trip. We filled the boat with water and the air-filled floatation bags did not stay in place, so the boat sank. A member of the team spent the next few days wedged into the boat, securely fastening the floatation to the appropriate spots for optimal stability. I never did get time to see if I could right the boat if she capsized.

Finally, I took her on a trip up the Intracoastal Waterway to spend the night. I had hoped to go up to a nice anchorage on the Manatee River, but a cold front was coming and I didn't want to be out in Tampa Bay if the weather turned really bad. I ducked behind an island up by Anna Maria and found a very shallow cove to anchor in by some homes. I figured if something went wrong, I could always walk to shore to get help. The boat was high and dry in the middle of the night, during the low tide. I would have to wait for the tide to come in to sail her out of the cove. This boat had a shallow draft. With the center-board raised up into the hull, there was only four inches of her underwater. This allowed me to go into very shallow water.

It took me forever to erect the tent, and I discovered that the snaps were placed so that I would have to be standing outside the boat to completely finish snapping it down. This was rectified. I also decided that I needed some kind of cushion to lie on, as sleeping on the fiberglass deck for three months was going to get very uncomfortable. A local boat cushion company took pity on me and custom made two closed-cell cushions in red for visibility and safety's sake. I thanked them many a night when I cuddled down to sleep.

Prevail under power

The cold front came through in the middle of the night, bringing lots of lightning and wind, but very little rain. I didn't get much of a chance to see how weatherproof the tent was going to be. The next morning, I was very glad that I hadn't ventured out into Tampa Bay; the wind was howling! I surfed Sarasota Bay back to the sailing squadron. It was so windy that the races for the day had been cancelled.

I was pleased by the performance of the boat. However, between my work schedule, speaking engagements, and getting everything in my personal life settled to leave my home for three months, we never had a chance to test the flotation or go offshore into the Gulf of Mexico and test *Prevail* in the big water.

I also kept waiting on the agreement to be written. We had discussed what personal expenses needed to be paid and some of the safety concerns involved with the trip, but nothing had been put in writing. This was Ken's job and it was not at the top of the list due to all the other demands on his time. I was uncomfortable, and doubt had been creeping in. The follow-through had not been as good as I had expected and this was more of the same. I have learned in life that what may be at the top of my list may not be at the top of someone else's.

March also brought bad news. My mother was diagnosed with breast cancer and had to have a mastectomy. I took off work two weeks earlier than I'd planned so that I could be with her. We discussed the trip and whether I should go through with it due to her health. Since I would be in Florida for the first month at least, we decided I would go for it.

I could always leave the trip to go home at any time if she needed me.

The week prior to the trip was a nightmare. Not all of the equipment had been installed, and the agreement had still not been written. No arrangements had been made for money or a credit card; I didn't even have a cell phone. A friend of mine, David, came through and donated a cell phone to the cause at the last minute.

One bright spot in the week was an interview with Bob Hite, who was the news anchor on WFLA and a sailor to boot! He wanted to come out sailing with me on *Prevail* for an interview. The boat had been moved from Sarasota to St. Petersburg, so we could easily make the arrangements. I still laugh when I remember myself, Bob (who is a big guy), and his cameraman (also a big guy like Bob), all on tiny little *Prevail*. There was hardly room for us to move on the boat as we sailed around the St. Petersburg pier. I was proud of *Prevail* for being able to handle the weight and still get us safely back to the dock!

The agreement was finally written on the Sunday night before the trip. I was exhausted. Ken had chosen to spend the weekend crewing for a friend in a sailboat race instead of finishing the boat. I met with Ken in a classroom at the sailing center. He brought his computer and printer. He was in a foul mood, and mine was not much better.

The SPPD board had to put a lot of pressure on him to follow through with this chore. We were both under a lot of pressure; we had put our reputations and skills on the line for this venture. We had commitments to sponsors and sailors with disabilities. The tensions were high.

He had obviously put a lot of thought into the contract as it flowed off his computer. He'd put in there that I had to agree to follow the insurance rules. I asked what those were, since I had not previously been apprised of the insurance agreement. The biggest issue was that I couldn't sail after dark. This was going to make the trip tougher due to some of the distances between ports. SPPD would make my monthly mortgage, health insurance, car, and retirement account payments. They would also pay for trip expenses. We finally finished with an agreement we could both live with, and it was printed out and signed.

Another friend of mine, Jim Myers, had introduced me to Bobbi Grant a few weeks prior. I asked her if she would do all the communication for the trip. Bobbi and I spent hours going over email lists and logistics. Bobbi had been in marketing professionally before she retired. She turned out to be a phenomenal woman, an incredible liaison, as well as a great communicator.

Jim Myers also offered to follow me in his cabin cruiser for the first few days of the trip. I hadn't had time to pack *Prevail* due to the installation of the equipment not being completed in time for the sendoff, so I threw all of my gear into Jim's boat and decided to pack the boat on the way down the Intracoastal Waterway.

Finally, the big day arrived—April 11, 2000. The website was set up, an itinerary was made, and family, friends, sponsors, and the media came out to participate in the launch. My friend Daniel Davison from Naples had gotten in touch with CNN, and a journalist named Tim Wall came down to film the occasion. Turned out he wanted to document the entire trip!

The St. Pete Sunrise Rotary gave me breakfast as well as contacts along the way, then sent me off in grand style. Rotarians all up the East Coast of the U.S. were put on alert and were ready to help in any way that I needed. Mayor Fisher provided a proclamation that named April 11, 2000, as Alder Allensworth Day! What a wonderful feeling.

The Canadian Paralympic sailing team was out in force. They had been in St. Pete for the trials and I had been one of the volunteers assigned to them. What a great group of guys; they were one of my biggest cheering sections. It was all a blur, reporters with cameras and microphones shoved into my face, saying goodbye to my family, last-minute equipment being thrown onto Jim's boat, and friends galore on the dock wishing me well.

Bruce, a member of the St. Petersburg Yacht Club and Sunrise Rotary, gave the blessing. I took the bottle of champagne, a special boat-christening bottle donated by West Marine, and broke the bottle over the bow. A cheer went up, then it was time to get on board and go.

I hoisted the sail and in the light morning Tampa Bay breeze, I left St. Petersburg for the adventure of my life.

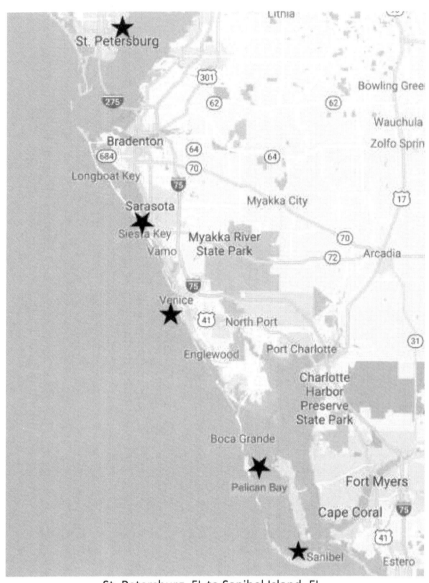

St. Petersburg, FL to Sanibel Island, FL

CHAPTER 9

The key is to have a dream that inspires us to go beyond our limits.

~

- Robert Kriegel -

St. Petersburg, Florida to Sanibel, Florida
April 11-April 17, 2000

I left the St. Petersburg city dock under sail. It seemed to take such a long time just to get out of the yacht basin. Once around the jetty though, I was free. I tried to determine the fastest route down Tampa Bay to the bridge at Anna Maria Island, but first, I had to take care of a personal problem.

My period had started that morning, so once I was out of sight of people, I had to take care of myself. I carried baby wipes, feminine hygiene products, and garbage bags, ready for any emergency. I also carried a female urinal and bottle to take care of nature's call.

I attempted to set the autopilot so that I could turn my full attention to my task, but it wouldn't work right. The boat kept going around in circles. I finally lashed the tiller down with a line, so I could use both hands. This seemed to work well temporarily. I put autopilot on the list of things to be worked on in Venice.

Approaching the Sunshine Skyway Bridge, I was overwhelmed looking up at its height and splendor. It made me realize just how small and vulnerable I was. Tim Wall from CNN was on the south fishing pier, ready to film as I sailed through the bridge. The water sparkled and the wind blew gently into my sails, keeping me on course across Tampa Bay.

Jim promised that he would come by, throw me an ice cream bar, and take a picture. He quickly overtook me and I got my ice cream. We figured that I was moving about three miles an hour; I can walk faster than that. It was going to be a long trip to Maine.

Jim, with Ken on board, went on ahead. The plan was to meet me at the Anna Maria Bridge at the entrance to Sarasota Bay. It was nice knowing I had an escort on the water to make sure I got where I was going. I was on a time limit to get to a dinner engagement in Sarasota, so they planned on towing me if we needed to increase the speed.

Another thing I'd done to prepare for the trip was to become a Toastmaster, as I knew that I would have to speak in front of people and be interviewed. The St. Petersburg chapter of Toastmasters, "Toast of the Bay," was a great group of people that met on Thursday mornings at 7:00 a.m. at Bayfront hospital. They were supportive and tough with me at the same time. As I was preparing for my interviews and speeches in Sarasota that night, I reflected on all they had taught me the last six months.

I reflected on all the incredibly supportive and generous people that had made this trip possible, people who were getting nothing in return. People who did not know if I would even accomplish the trip still gave from their hearts to make this dream happen. I would not let them down.

I wouldn't let the people with disabilities in my community down, either. I was doing this for them. Why shouldn't all people be able to enjoy the beautiful waters that surround Pinellas County and our entire country? It would just take a little technology, and they, too, would be able to join the rest of us able-bodied people in the pleasure of sailing.

This was such a small task that I had taken on compared with what it took for someone with a disability just to make it through the day. I got to have fun while doing something important for others at the same time. I love a win/win situation.

I finally made it to the bridge and it was obvious that if left to my own power, I would not make to Sarasota until the next day. Jim took me under tow and as we accelerated across the bay, Ken briefed me on what was expected of me when we arrived. I just wanted to relax and enjoy the ride before I was put out into the public eye that night, but it was business first!

Finally, we got to the dock at the Sarasota Yacht Club. The harbormaster had set aside room at the dock for me in my own boat slip. I took a shower and put on a skirt, blouse, and heels, the one nice outfit I had packed for the trip just for occasions such as these. Pictures were taken on the dock with me dressed to the nines beside the boat. It was very incongruous.

The reception I received was wonderful, and I was riding on a high as I spent not a very restful first night of the trip on the boat. It was a private club, so there was not much in the way of people wandering around, and it was in a protected area, so there wasn't much boat traffic. It was my mind and excitement that kept me awake.

The next morning, I got up early to take the boat over to Marina Jack for breakfast, another interview, and a sendoff. I got my first taste of congested waterways on my way over, picking my way between pleasure boats, fishing boats, jet skis, and wakes.

By the time I got to the dock, I had been completely bounced around and was very glad to see friends and a priest waiting for me to land. We had breakfast, then I went out to board the boat. The priest gave me a St. Christopher that he had blessed, and a cross. To this day, I keep that St. Christopher in my lifejacket and the cross in my wallet. I know that the strength of God is always with me.

I pushed off into the bay and headed south. Tim Wall was on a powerboat close behind and took pictures of me sailing down the waterway toward Venice.

I decided to stay in the Intracoastal Waterway instead of going out through Sarasota Big Pass. It would take too long to go out the pass and then have to come back in. It was a beautiful sail and I didn't have to use the engine, so I could make it to the dock by nightfall.

I arrived at Venice and was put at the dinghy dock. Jim was already there in his powerboat. I made sure my boat was fast to the dock and that everything was put away shipshape before I made my way into the bar at the Venice Yacht Club. I walked into the bar and people started to clap, then they gave me a standing ovation. I was stunned. I didn't know what to do. I just started to smile, shake hands, and thank them. It was incredible.

People bought me drinks and I talked about my journey up to that point and told them what I wanted to accomplish on the trip. People wanted a tour of the boat. That took all of two minutes! The Venice-Nokomis Rotary had also invited me to dinner that evening and I gave a talk about the trip.

The next night, Joe, who owned the Nautical Trader, a chandlery, and writes the newsletter for the sailing squadron, invited me to speak at the Venice Sailing Squadron and participate in their potluck dinner. He also invited me to his store to pick out anything that I still needed for the trip. There were a couple things on the list and we made plans for him to pick me up the next morning and help me get supplies, including extra fuel and food.

That night, I slept on the floor of Jim's boat, as they predicted rain. I was glad I did, because it was a gully washer that night. I did not have to deal with taking down and drying out a wet tent. I got up rested and ready to meet Ken to install more of the equipment, look at the auto helm, and decide what to pack on the boat. I was also hoping Ken had some money for me, as I was very short of cash. I had several interviews scheduled with newspapers and TV stations. We planned for a couple of days in Venice to finish outfitting the boat before I struck out on my own.

That evening, we went to the potluck dinner at The Venice Sailing Squadron. It was wonderful, and they had another surprise waiting, a donation to SPPD. Once again, the big hearts of the people I met shone through. I knew right then that I was on the right path.

Ken left without leaving me any money. He had not gotten the boat registered, although it's mandatory to have a boat registered if it has an engine. I was now at risk for being pulled over and given a ticket. I received one more email before I left the dock, a message from Daniel Davison's friend Bob in Naples. Daniel had $100 and the boat registration for me. Finally, Ken had come through.

They told me to come in through Gordon Pass in Naples and they would be waiting for me in a powerboat to escort me to a dock for the night. The dock was behind a private residence, and the owner, Prudence, a retired schoolteacher, had a dry bed waiting.

They asked if there was anything I needed for the boat in Naples. Ken had not been able to work on the auto helm, so I asked for someone who knew something about marine electronics. They had just the man for the job, saying he put MacGyver to shame.

I had time to read a few of the well-wishing emails from SPPD's website. My friend and fellow sailor Randy built and managed it. Randy had been in a head-on collision (not his fault) and lost both of his legs. He had joined SPPD for the therapy and stuck around to become a Paralympic sailor. It was always such fun to watch the unsuspecting crowd as Randy would sail his 2.4-meter boat to the dock with his legs sticking out of the cockpit behind him. It warmed my heart to have so many friends rooting for me!

I left Venice Yacht Club early on April 15 and figured it would take me three days to get to Naples. I was now getting ready to take off into little-known territory, really on my own. Jim was headed back to St. Petersburg and I was headed south. I planned to spend the first night at anchor in Pelican Bay and then head on to Captiva and Sanibel for my second night, then onto Naples on the 17th, to arrive in the afternoon.

I was a little nervous, but also excited with anticipation. The next morning, I listened to the weather report. The call was for another beautiful day in paradise. As I pulled out into the Intracoastal, I reflected on my time in Venice. I had received a call from a woman who had also been diagnosed with cancer of the lacrimal gland 12 years before. I was stunned. The doctors had told me that they didn't know of anyone who had ever survived the diagnosis. She stated that she'd had the radical surgery and that it was the only cure to her knowledge.

Here I was in Venice, Florida, embarking upon the journey of a lifetime, talking to another survivor. This I took as God's way of saying that I was going to survive this journey and touch many hearts along the way. I knew that many people would touch my heart, too.

It was time to head south to Pelican Bay. I had a tank full of gas, food, and water. Food meant canned goods, power bars, apples, and cheese. I also had green tea bags that I could use to make sun tea along the way. I had a jar of honey to add to the tea for a bit of sweetness and energy. That was enough to make it three days to Naples.

The boat was loaded with my small one-burner stove, food, water, fuel, toiletries, safety gear, electronics, a solar panel, and batteries, so it was sitting low in the water. Personal gear included one nice-looking outfit for the "occasions" along the way, two nice *Prevail* shirts, shorts, a couple of old pairs of shorts and T-shirts for every day, and a couple of swimsuits. I also had about seven pairs of nice cotton underwear. There is no better ending to a tough wet day on the water than nice dry cotton underwear.

I had my Tilley hat and my father's old long-sleeve white Navy uniform shirts to protect my torso and arms from the sun. My sailing gloves protected the palms of my hands from the lines and the back of my hands from the sun. I had noticed the tops of my legs were burning and wasn't sure how to address that issue. Sunscreen wasn't enough. A towel covering was hot.

***

The trip from Venice to Pelican Bay was challenging. The wind was on the nose most of the way. But isn't this the lot of most sailors? The wind is always coming from where you want to go. The more determined you are to get there, the stronger the winds and waves are against you. This was going to test me and let me see what the boat and I were made of.

I also still had my safety net, as I was within radio contact of Jim's boat, the good ship *Spice*. The weather wasn't bad by sailor's standards, but it was the worst so far on the trip. The wind was blowing 15-20 knots from the south and there was a one to two foot chop on the bay. And did I say it was on the nose?

Pelican Bay is a little bit of a pristine paradise away from the tourist crowds. It's nestled behind the island of Cayo Costa, which is a state park, and far enough away from the mainland that it can only be accessed by boat. The anchorage at Pelican Bay is perfect, very protected, and has plenty of deep water. There are also lots of friendly manatee, and beautiful sunsets. The beaches on the island are almost deserted, and there is a small reef on the gulf side that can be visited by snorkelers.

When I arrived, I was surprised to see *Spice* anchored in the bay. I thought Jim was headed back north. He had decided to come to Pelican Bay instead, a favorite anchorage, since he was so close. He suggested I raft my boat alongside, but I wanted the independence of being secured under my own anchor and making sure everything was working as it should. He provided dinner, as my rations were meager.

I relished the nice evening meal and glass of wine. Afterwards, I went to my boat for my first night of the trip sleeping on it at anchor. I put up my tent, which covered the entire deck, and lay down on my red pad with my sleeping bag that I pulled out from one of the storage compartments. The storage compartments were tight and the edges sharp. As I pulled the gear out, I cut up my hand. I bandaged it and went to sleep.

The next morning, after I'd had a great swim and rinsed off with my solar shower, Jim called me over for breakfast. We looked over the chart and I figured out how to get to the dock at Captiva. No more delays; this was it. I was off alone to conquer the coast for people with disabilities, or so my inflated ego thought.

Another beautiful day in paradise, I decided to cut across the flats instead of going the long way around, through the channel. I saw fishing boats out there, so with my boat only drawing four inches with the board up, no problem. I didn't get very far before I ran aground. No problem. Get out and drag her off.

My weight getting out of the boat was enough to refloat her, and I grabbed the painter (a line connected to the bow of the boat to be used for towing or to tie up to a dock) and walked to deeper water. Once back onboard, I went to start the motor as the wind was getting lighter. I gave a prayer of thanks for having a motor.

The motor didn't start. I made sure that the choke and handle throttle were in the right place, then pulled the cord again. No response. Now I was drifting with the tide. Did I throw the anchor or just drift? It shouldn't take long to get her started. Oh, check the gas. Silly me; maybe I had run out. I wasn't sure how long a tank lasted, and that could be the problem ... nope, plenty of gas.

I carried a five-gallon gas can in the cockpit at my feet. The tank on top of the engine held one gallon at a time. I was going to have to time a tank and see how long it lasted.

So, what next? My extensive knowledge of small motor repair had just run out. I know! I took off my T-shirt and starting waving it at the flats fishermen, wearing just my bikini top and shorts. A non-emergency emergency call! It didn't take long for help to arrive.

His first question was, did I have enough gas? I gave him that look of "Don't insult me; I'm smarter than that." The second question was, had I checked the spark plug?

Okay, I gave him that one, and I should have thought of it myself. He pulled out his wrench, I found mine, and I was given a quick lesson on un-fouling spark plugs. The engine started up like a charm. I gave him my best smile and wished him good fishing.

I started making my way down to Captiva. It was such a beautiful area. The bay was big enough and shallow enough to discourage the congestion of boaters. My company was the gulls, pelicans, and a few flats fishermen in the distance. Even a few dolphins came up for air, just to check me out.

Jim radioed that he had decided to head to Captiva, instead of home, since he was in the area. He said the dock master, a woman, wanted to meet me. I easily found the channel to Captiva and made my way to the yacht club dock. The dock master wasn't there that day, but Jim treated me to a nice lunch at the yacht club.

I went over to the fuel dock to top up my five-gallon can, having figured that one gallon of gas lasted about one hour. There was a small crowd of mostly kids at the fuel dock, and as I got closer, I discovered what the excitement was all about. There was a family of otters putting on a show.

Close to the dock was an anchorage for transient sailors, and a few old-timers lived aboard. "The water is free" was their motto. I saw a small dinghy leave a battered-looking sailboat and make its way toward us at the dock. As they approached, they called the name of my ship and I waved to them.

One of the gentlemen in the dinghy handed me a $20 bill and thanked me for sailing for people with disabilities, telling me he wanted to contribute to the cause. Tears welled up in my eyes. I could not believe the generosity.

He said that he and his brother had been out here sailing around and had heard about the trip. He'd felt compelled to help. Before he turned to leave, I told him this money would pay for gas and food for the next leg of my trip.

I got back on my boat, waved goodbye to Jim, and with a warm heart, started out by myself to find a place in Sanibel to stay for the night.

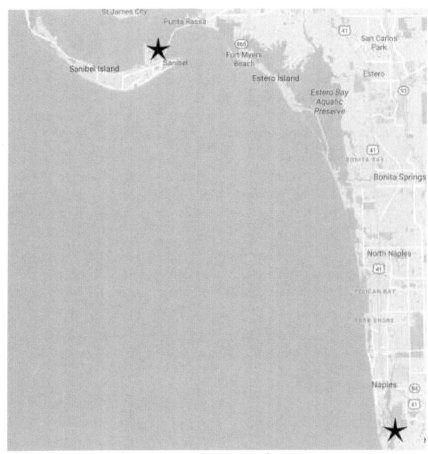

Sanibel Island, FL to Naples, FL

CHAPTER 10

No amount of skill, no equipment, and no boat will keep you from disaster if you don't develop the most important seagoing skill of all, a complete fear of falling overboard.

~

- Lin and Larry Pardey -

Sanibel Island, Florida to Naples, Florida
April 17 to April 20, 2000

The breeze was finally in my favor for an afternoon run to Sanibel. As I got closer to the island, the bay narrowed, deepened, and the boat traffic increased. This was the playground of the power boaters and tourists of the West Coast. There was a wonderful wide channel out into the gulf for those who were into fishing and diving, and in the bay, boat ramps, marinas, fuel docks, and restaurants. In my boat, I felt a bit small. I went up one of the channels to a marina to find a place to dock for the night and top off the fuel tank, but it was too crowded.

I had been sailing most of the afternoon, so I hadn't used much fuel. I knew that I would be offshore the next day, so I wouldn't have as much need for the engine. I decided that four gallons should be plenty for the trip to Naples. After all, this was a sailboat, not a motorboat.

I headed back up the channel and threw out my anchor close to the boat ramp at the county park. I was just inside the main bridge over to the island. I would sail under the same bridge into the open gulf in the morning. I sat on the deck watching the thunderclouds build over the mainland, and eating my evening power bar.

I pulled out a fresh bottle of water and shoved a teabag in it to infuse for breakfast the next morning, then erected my tent. Once again, I tried to figure out how to get my sleeping bag out of the compartment without further abusing my injured hand. No such luck. Good thing I had plenty of Band-Aids in my first aid kit.

I spent a restless night being serenaded by the roar of boat engines, entertained by the lightning flashing across the sky, and rocked by the wake of fishing boats. What a way to start my first part of the journey alone.

I must have slept some, because I became aware of getting hotter and hotter as the morning sun baked into the dark blue tent and the gulls started fighting over breakfast. I got up and dismantled the tent, pushing it back into its storage hole. I became aware of what a hassle and time waster setting up and putting away the tent was. I also became aware of how much room it took up in the boat. I knew that there would be times I would be thankful for it, so I put up with the inconvenience.

Time to eat my apple, drink my green tea with honey, and head out to sea. I sailed under the bridge across San Carlos Bay out into the Gulf of Mexico. I was very apprehensive, as it was my first time offshore in the dinghy. I didn't know how she would handle heavy seas. My cockpit wasn't self-bailing, and I didn't know for sure if she would float full of water. Air bags had been secured in her after the failed test, but we had never retested.

There are really no navigable passes between Sanibel and Naples. I just had to go for it, the moment of no return. I was alone, offshore with only God, my half-tested skills, and the boat. It was a beautiful morning, and I gave thanks. A perfect 8-knot easterly morning breeze was blowing from the shore, and I was on a reach headed south.

I watched the fishing boats and tourist boats coming out for a day on the water. I enjoyed the gulls and the pelicans diving ahead of me. Pelicans are amazing; they look so big and awkward, but fly with such grace, so adapted to their environment. I envied them. We humans, on the other hand, have lost this ability to easily adapt due to our sheltered lifestyle. I have always fancied learning to survive off the sea and the land, but have never taken the steps to learn.

It's much more convenient to go to the mall and buy clothes, and go to the grocery store and buy food. I'm so dependent on others. This dependency scares me sometimes. It's a strength of ours to be able to work together and provide for each other, but also a downfall to be so dependent on others for our every need.

I didn't even know how to fix the motor on my boat; I couldn't get the auto helm to work properly. So, I needed experts in all fields around me just to survive. Would I be able to master these skills, or did I even need them in order to make the trip successful?

Have we become so enamored with technology that we think that we can't live without it? My first plan for the trip had been not to have an engine, but to have oars. Some very seasoned sailors had quickly talked me out of this. It was still my hope not to use the engine very much.

As I was contemplating these issues and solving other world problems in my mind, I noticed a few waves coming from the west. Now this was strange, as the wind was still out of the east. I looked around to see if any big boats had gone by; I sure didn't hear any. No boats on the horizon.

The waves seemed to be consistent: long and gentle. I looked at my position on the GPS and marked it on my paper chart, then looked at the coastline and the time, making sure that everything added up. I was on course and about one third of the way to Naples, making good time under sail.

Something, though, kept nagging me about these waves from the wrong direction, so I turned on the weather radio and learned that a cold front was approaching. Not a cloud in the sky above me, and a nice breeze carrying me south. As noon approached, the wind died and the seas became more confused. I ate a little lunch: a power bar and some water, as the sea breeze came in I jibed the sail and set up on a reach on the opposite tack going south.

The seas continued to build, and I started seeing a few fluffy clouds coming in from the northwest. I always thought of such clouds as the advance troops in an army before the main force came in. I was starting to get a little nervous.

Did I say that there were no decent passes between Sanibel and Naples? My only choice would be to beach the boat if worst came to worst. Whatever that was? Did I say that the cockpit was not self-bailing, and I didn't know for sure that she wouldn't sink? Where was that lifejacket with the blessed St. Christopher in it? I found it stuffed under the tent.

I lashed the tiller down. With the boat on a reach, it would pretty much hold course by itself for a few minutes at a time so that I could let go of the helm. I only had to reach over adjust the helm occasionally to make a slight correction. I dug out the tent and then the jacket—not a great place to keep my life jacket. I made a mental note to always have it on top. I put the jacket on and checked my safety equipment on the bow.

I double-checked all the emergency supplies ARC had donated and made sure that everything was where it would be available and easily detachable from the boat if it went down. I reefed my main sail down one. This was so easy to do with the donated Dutchman system, even in a boat that was being lifted and dropped in the waves.

The winds freshened to 15 knots with gusts to 20 knots. The seas grew to three to five feet. I tried to keep panic away by making preparations like, did I have water and food in my emergency bag, just in case? Finally, after running out of things to do, I untied the helm and steered a straight course for Naples Pass. As the seas continued to build, I thought about all the times I had raced boats in the bay and offshore.

Other instances of rough weather and frightening experiences started running through my head as the seas and wind continued to build. I knew how quickly the weather could change offshore, and there was no place to run and hide. I could feel my free hand gripping the gunwale of the boat as I held her on course with the other. She wasn't overpowered and was sailing along smartly. She even seemed to enjoy running up and down the waves. My fingers, though, were making impressions in the fiberglass.

I have raced windsurfers for years and had wiped out on many an occasion. You just get up on the board, pull the sail out of the water, and go again. You're usually close to a shore and there are other people around. There was not a soul or a boat close by now!

Jacquie Albina's words echoed in my mind: "I don't swim." I was taking those words to heart; they became my mantra. I sailed as conservatively as I could to make it safely to Naples.

As I neared Gordon Pass, the gateway to Naples, I could see the boats going in and out of the channel. The waves were so huge in the pass that some of the smaller boats disappeared in the troughs. With the tide going out and the wind coming in, the waves were starting to stack up.

I knew my friend Daniel Davison was meeting me on the water once I was through the pass, I just had to get through!

Daniel is missing parts of all four extremities from severe frostbite, due to passing out on the ice from a drug overdose in Chicago. He now spends his time talking to kids about staying drug free and inspiring others to live life to the fullest, despite such a crippling injury. After the injury, he learned to sail and it has been very healing for him. I feel the same way about sailing.

Daniel had also hooked me up with Tim Wall to help me promote the trip. I was really looking forward to seeing Daniel, but I was really looking forward to making it safely through the pass first!

I was watching the boat traffic and didn't want to be in the pass when a big fishing boat went through. I watched as a large sailboat, well over 35 feet, entered the pass. The waves were bouncing it around like crazy.

All of a sudden it was over, broaching, and the boom hit the water. It came back up with the skipper fighting the helm, water streaming off the stern.

A knockdown like that would probably be the end of my boat and maybe of me. With the cockpit not self-bailing, I didn't think I could right her, full of gear, in the waves by myself. I had never practiced that skill on the *Prevail*, though I had done it plenty of times on sunfish, Hobie Cats, and my Coronado 15.

I started to explore my other options. I could sail on down to Marco Island and go through that pass instead, but it might not be any better. I could sail through the smaller waves and beach her, but then how would I get her fully loaded off the beach? I could just keep on sailing and hope to hit some solid ground somewhere east of Key West. Or I could just stop looking at the other options and sail through the pass.

The worst thing that could happen was sinking and dying.

I lined up on the sea buoy and started my approach. There was no traffic in the pass. I started to run through all I knew about preventing a broach as I eased the sail out for the downwind run. I made ready to spill air by fully releasing the sail and vang and pointing up a couple of degrees if I had to. I moved my weight further back in the boat to decrease any weather helm. I think I even gripped the gunwale tighter if possible, and put her bow into the first wave.

The *Prevail* rode right up it and surfed down the other side. Here came the next wave, riding to the top, hesitating for a second, and a great surf to the bottom. And once again, each time a brief hesitation on the top and a great surf to the bottom. Then I was through the pass into calm water. Releasing my grip, I closed my eyes and said a prayer of thanksgiving.

I opened my eyes just in time to see a 40-foot sport fisherman, fondly referred to as a "stinkpot" by sailors, coming full speed around the corner and throwing a huge wake into my boat. As I sat there bailing, I realized that I had dealt with Mother Nature, but the stinkpot, which is the bane—or is that the vain—of man's existence, almost sank me there in the calm waters of Naples Harbor.

After getting most of the water out of the boat and drying off, I headed up the channel toward Naples. Daniel and Bob had commandeered a powerboat and met me in the Naples River as promised. They escorted me to Prudence's home and dock. It was wonderful to be at a safe harbor after such a hair-raising sail.

We had a lovely dinner and then Prudence took me over to the house of a friend, Regina, who wanted to meet me. Regina had a hot tub and we spent a girls' evening soaking, drinking wine, and solving all of the world's problems.

I had an appointment the next day with the renowned Naples MacGyver, boat electronics guru Jim. A local boat captain with extensive knowledge of the Everglades, he quoted Lin and Larry Parday to me: "If you can't repair it, maybe it shouldn't be on board."

Lin and Larry are well-known blue water cruisers and writers. Most sailors I know have studied their books extensively before taking offshore cruises.

I just happened to be sailing the most technically advanced 12-foot boat in existence. I had two GPS units, one mounted and one handheld, both with C-map capability and chart chips, a handheld radio, a mounted radio, an EPIRB, and an auto helm. On the other hand, I myself wasn't very technologically advanced. Changing a spark plug successfully and creating a route on the hand-held GPS were my only claims to fame.

Arriving exhausted at Naples one week into a long voyage made me determined to learn how to use the auto helm. My meager attempts in the past had found the boat sailing in circles when I would push the engage button. So far, I had only used it, unengaged, as a rigid bar to hold the helm steady for a few minutes so I could take care of necessary chores. It wasn't reliable for more than a few minutes, though, and I would find myself sailing wildly off course.

Jim, the handsome electronics guru arrived looking rather like an Indiana Jones; I had probably been at sea too long. He immediately asked for the manuals, not wasting any words on common courtesies. It was going to be a long day. After a careful study of the manuals while the rest of us enjoyed lemonade by the pool, he looked at me and said, "Let's take her for a spin."

I had taken everything off the boat to clean it, so I quickly grabbed a couple of lifejackets as he leapt aboard. Now, there isn't much room in a 12-foot boat, and we were soon uncomfortably cozy, his good looks and casual confidence overwhelming me. He said that we had to calibrate the auto helm, and a few other words that would take an engineering degree to interpret. I smiled and asked him what I needed to do.

He told me to start the engine and take us out to a wide place in the waterway. We needed to turn large, slow circles to accomplish our task. I headed out while he pushed buttons to set up the auto helm. We made lots of wide circles and then would try straight for a ways. He finally convinced the machine to drive the boat in the direction I needed to go. He gave me a simple explanation and asked me to try it on my own.

While practicing with the auto helm, Jim asked me about my sail plan through the Everglades to Key Largo. He warned me off of navigating through the Ten Thousand Islands. He said that all the mangrove islands started to look alike and you could easily lose your way.

We discovered that there were no computer chip maps, aka c-maps, for the section from Flamingo to Key Largo. This area is not on the usual navigational charts, as it is a crocodile sanctuary and very shallow. Only the locals go there to fish. Jim joked about an Indian tribe of midgets who perpetually wandered about the mangroves, jumping up and down and shouting their tribal name, "Wheretheheckrwee."

Jim told me to follow the Intracoastal Waterway south to Marathon and go east along the Keys. He said that I wouldn't get lost that way and that there would be people nearby in case I needed help. This route would take me several extra days. I had really wanted to cut due east from Flamingo to Key Largo, but he strongly discouraged it, and also suggested that I stock up on lots of water and fuel, as there was nothing available from when I left Goodland until I got to the Keys.

Jim went forward, all of five feet away, and looked at my mounted GPS, then turned and asked me how I liked the unit. I confessed that I hadn't used it because I didn't really know how to work it; I relied on my handheld. I also dead-reckoned along the coast, so there had been no need. He shot me a disgusted look and started to punch more buttons, fixing it so I could see my heading and speed from a distance. At least I still had the boat headed in a straight line.

Then suddenly, the engine quit. I reset the throttle and pulled the cord. Nothing. Repeatedly, I tried to restart the motor, hoping a wave would come up and swallow me. There was no other way out. He came to the stern and took off the gas cap. No gas. I realized that in my haste, I hadn't picked up my spare can. Jim looked at me and smiled; my heart melted.

He said this was the first time a lady had ever taken him out for a ride and run out of gas. Where was that wave to swallow me up when I needed it? I didn't even have a paddle on board. Talk about feeling like you were up the proverbial creek.

No problem, as we could sail back to the dock, against the wind and tide. I must admit, I couldn't have planned it better; we did have a fun time sailing the boat back. There is something about being under sail that brings out the best in any situation.

My friend Daniel wanted to know if we had been successful in fixing the autopilot and I said yes, it was a very successful trip. Jim asked if he could look at the GPS manual, and I rummaged in my dry box for it. Assuming a pedantic air, he asked if I had read the manuals. I said they were a sure-fire cure for insomnia and that I had not gotten along with them very well.

As he left, he said there were two things I needed when I started through the Everglades: peanut M&M's and RFM. Curious, I asked for an explanation. He said that M&M's are a great adjunct to the short rations I was going to be on for my week in the wilderness, and RFM stood for Read the F____ Manuals.

I saluted and smiled, hoping that one day in the not-too-distant future, I might run out of gas with him again.

The other issue I had to deal with was my sunburned thighs. I could not keep enough sunscreen on them to keep them from burning. I didn't want to wear long pants, as they would be hot and take up too much room in my boat.

Daniel and I then made a trip to Sam's Club where I bought several cases of water, peanut M&M's, and a second five-gallon gas can.

I also found a pair of pink nylon pajama bottoms. They were perfect for the trip, lightweight, dried easily, and would protect my legs. I could pull them over my shorts or swimsuit.

I must have been a sight in my sailing costume. My father's old long-sleeve white uniform shirts, pink pajama bottoms, and my Tilley hat. That, plus all the sponsors on the hull and the sail, I must have looked like an eccentric aquatic NASCAR driver.

I stocked up on apples, cheese, green tea, and power bars. I still had my soup and my little stove. I should be fine for the week it would take me to sail through the Everglades.

Daniel had set up interviews for us with the local TV stations and newspapers. He was starting a sailing program for people with disabilities in Naples, and we were able to get more interest generated for him and his mission. The people I had met in Naples were absolutely wonderful and so helpful to me.

It was time for me to pack the boat and continue my journey south. I was really looking forward to this leg of the journey, both with excitement and a bit of healthy apprehension.

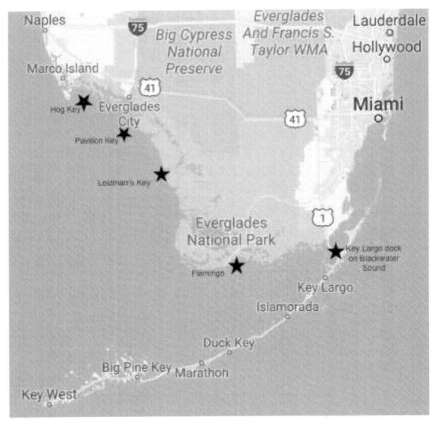

Naples, FL to Key Largo, FL

CHAPTER 11

The future belongs to those who believe in the beauty of their dreams.

~

- Eleanor Roosevelt -

Naples, Florida to Key Largo, Florida
April 20 to April 26, 2000

It was Thursday, April 20. I left my support group at the dock in Naples and headed south down the Intracoastal Waterway toward Marco Island. My boat was loaded. I had an extra fuel tank, loads of water, and food. After Goodland, less than two hours away, I would not see a store or a marina for the next week.

Marco Island was the winter playground of the wealthy. I passed incredible homes and condos with very expensive boats at the docks. I wondered what all of those people did for a living to make that kind of money. It astounded me; wealth in one area, and then, just barely next door, poverty.

Goodland leaned more to the poorer side. As I rounded the bend, I saw the liveaboards at anchor; this was the jumping off place to the Keys and beyond. There wasn't much land or beach to attract tourists. Goodland was the gateway to the Ten Thousand Islands, mainly mangroves and marina, which attracted fishermen and sailors who wanted to live frugally off the sea.

It was about noon, and I stopped at a little marina to top up the gas tank one last time. The marina had seen better days, but there was plenty of activity. I was a bit nervous about leaving the shelter of the Intracoastal again after my last experience offshore in the Gulf. I queried the dock master as to the conditions in Florida Bay. He was not very inspiring.

He was downright concerned about me going out into Florida Bay in that little boat. I had sailed through some of the worst storms in my life on Florida Bay, and I knew what that shallow water could do when the weather turned nasty. There were not many choices other than go forward or quit, so go forward it was.

I sailed out Coon Key Pass, and as I left Coon Key behind, a pod of dolphins surfaced on my starboard side and welcomed me to Florida Bay. My spirits soared; it was going to be just fine. Whenever I saw a dolphin, I knew I would be protected.

I thought about another time the appearance of dolphins heralded safety. Two friends, Lillian and Wendy, and I were delivering a J-24 sailboat to a race in Clearwater, Florida. We were sailing the boat from St. Petersburg Yacht Club to Clearwater Yacht Club. The day was perfect, sunny and warm, with a following wind and sea. We knew a cold front was coming down from the north, one that had spawned tornados in Georgia. We hoped to make it to Clearwater before the front reached us.

We were just north of John's Pass, about 12 miles south of Clearwater, when we saw the black line on the horizon and the seas started to get confused. We doused the jib and put the motor on the back of the boat. The main sail didn't reef.

I called for lifejackets, emergency gear, and rain jackets to be brought topside. The storm hit with a vengeance and we couldn't get the outboard started. We could hardly see a boat length in front of us through the driving rain. I sent Wendy to the bow to call the waves and Lillian went to work trimming the main.

We had two choices: keep sailing to Clearwater, or turn and make a run for John's Pass. I knew I could sail through Clearwater Pass. I didn't think I could manage the drawbridge at John's Pass without an engine in the waves. We chose to beat into the wind and waves.

We would sail in as close to shore as we dared, then Wendy would watch for a flat spot in the waves, call it, and we would tack back out to sea. Lillian would dump the main when we were heeling over too far, and then power it up to punch through the next set of waves. This went on for what seemed like hours.

We finally saw the jetty at Clearwater Pass and a pod of dolphins playing in the waves. We gave a collective sigh of relief as we made the turn and surfed safely into Clearwater Bay.

So, dolphins welcoming me into Florida Bay today was a good omen. I sailed southeast toward Hog Key, my planned anchorage for the night.

The Keys, for me, are a place of wonder; I have always been romanced by their harsh beauty for the 20+ years I've been going there to fish, dive, and just be. When I catch a glimpse of a mangrove island, the tension in my shoulders releases about six notches.

I have lived long enough to see the devastation caused by man on these last wild outposts. The sugar plantations with their fertilizer runoff, along with the alteration of water and fill land for homes, have caused these wild habitats to deteriorate. Man wants immediate gratification and is sacrificing his future to get it.

Hog Key has a little known anchorage behind it, and I was the only one there that day. I ate my dinner of cold organic chili out of the can, with a peanut M&M chaser. Cooking on the deck with a propane burner on a 12-foot boat, with 10 gallons of fuel in the cockpit, was not a good idea. The propane burner would be left in Miami. I was becoming primitive!

After my chili, I got out the manuals and settled in for an evening of RFM. They were sure to put me to sleep.

***

The next morning, I arose to an incredible sunrise over Florida Bay. The early morning gulls welcomed the new day, diving into the opulent waters for their breakfast. I foraged for some fruit, and made a bottle of sun tea to get my day started. I was headed to Indian Key, just south of Everglades City, to meet a companion with his own sailboat for the rest of the journey to Flamingo.

I had been in contact with Steve Morrill from St. Petersburg, who frequently sailed his boat through the Everglades, and he'd offered to meet me at Indian Key, just at the end of the channel out of

Chokoloskee. Steve, a journalist and an avid sailor, had seen me speak at a Bay Sailor's meeting in Clearwater and asked if he could join me for this part of the journey. He even brought his own boat and provisions.

Steve had many years of experience as a guide in the Ten Thousand Islands and is the author of a murder mystery series set in the Everglades. He wanted to sail beside me. I had mixed feelings about this. I didn't know him, and the Everglades is a lonely place. If something happened to a single girl, they might never recover the body or learn of the deed. I also knew the pros and cons of having another person to look out after, but he could also look after me. He had the local knowledge I lacked.

This trip was about being open to whatever came my way. So, since the dolphins had already given their blessing of protection, I sailed toward Indian Key with great confidence.

Indian Key is the southernmost island at the end of Indian Pass, the gateway to Everglades City and the Everglades Wilderness Waterway, which connects Everglades City to Flamingo. Only accessible by boat, it's part of the Waterway and the Everglades National Park System and has a designated campground for people wanting to enjoy the peacefulness of the area. The National Park Service only allows so many passes per day on the Waterway to help maintain its natural beauty.

Steve and I met just as planned in the pass and continued our sail southeast to Pavilion Key, where we anchored for the night. His boat was a 21-foot Sea Pearl, which looked like a large canoe with two sails. He had a small engine and could also row the vessel. It made a beautiful picture as it cut through the water.

We landed on shore in a pile of fornicating horseshoe crabs. You could hardly walk and not step on them. They looked so prehistoric, with their hard brown shells and sharp spiked tails, coupled together on the beach. The old mariners would come here and harvest clams to sell further north, and the evidence of years of clamming helped to build up this little island.

Steve formally introduced himself and told me about the island, pointing out the most predominant landmark, a Porta-Potty up on the highest point of the clamshell island, and we took turns relieving ourselves.

Pavilion Key had a sordid history, and Steve told me how it got its name. A woman was murdered on the island and her body was placed on a "pavilion" that had been built on the island. The man who killed her was caught and hanged.

I'll anchor away from the island, I thought as I shivered a bit.

As darkness fell along with the tide, we pushed our vessels off into the anchorage to find good holding for the night. I was quite envious as I saw Steve quickly raise his tent over his boat and settle down with a peanut butter and jelly sandwich in less than 10 minutes, while I struggled for an hour putting up my tent for the night, and fell asleep too tired to bother with opening another can of cold chili.

During the night as the tide went out, I was aware that the rocking of the boat had ceased, and the wind had come up. There were strange noises all around me. I turned on the flashlight to be greeted by a raccoon taking advantage of the tide pulling all of the water out of the anchorage to look for a midnight snack. I just glared at him, turned over, and went back to sleep.

The next morning, I woke up to another beautiful sunrise and more neighbors. A man in a rowboat had come into the anchorage. This was one of those double-ended old-fashioned lifeboats you would see off of Cape Cod in the summertime. He had left from New York Harbor, rowed through the rivers across to the Mississippi, down through the delta, and along the west coast of Florida. He was on his way to Key West. He was doing this just to do it, and his goal was to finish back in New York Harbor. He, too, had peanut butter and jelly sandwiches.

This was the meal du jour of the waterway traveler. I needed to get with the diet plan.

Steve just as quickly disassembled his tent and made his boat ready to sail. My takedown time was longer. We could feel the wind blowing over the island, saw the waves breaking into the trees, and knew that we were in for a rough ride. It didn't take us long to come out from behind the island into the fray.

Steve told me we should sail close to shore as the waves were less, and I took his advice. I could see Steve's boat being bounced around in the waves. My boat felt as stable as a cork, taking each wave into stride, even enjoying it. The difference was in design and weight; my boat was designed to be a cork even while fully loaded with provisions.

Steve made a run for the shelter of a little no-name mangrove island to take a lunch break, then we decided to press on to Lostman's for the night.

Lostman's Key, at the mouth of Lostman's River, offered a nicely sheltered anchorage and beach. I got in close and took advantage of the brackish water to wash the worst of the salt off of my boat and sleeping pads. I did a little laundry and hung it up on the rigging to dry. I also pulled out my mosquito netting.

Bruce, of Sunrise Rotary, had asked me if I was going to take a jungle hammock with me. He'd used one when he was stationed in Vietnam, describing it as a sleeping bag covered by mosquito netting which could be strung up between trees. I'd bought the mosquito netting to cover my sleeping bag, but had not used it yet. I decided to try it instead of the tent tonight, as there was no rain in the forecast.

Resting on the beach, Steve told me the story of "Bloody" Ed Watson. Apparently, Watson had owned a sugar plantation in the area at the beginning of the 20th century.

He'd found two squatters when he was making the rounds of his "empire" in the Glades near Lostman's Key. The alleged squatters were a husband and wife trying to eke a living out of the Everglades. Bloody Ed apparently shot them first and didn't ask any questions.

About the same time, a hurricane went through and some more bodies turned up. Some of the bodies were found disemboweled and weighted down underwater. These were the bodies of people that had worked for him on the plantation.

The town's people at Chokoloskee were afraid of Bloody Ed, but also wanted him dead. Bloody Ed tried to lay the blame of the deaths on his foreman, Leslie Cox. He came back to town saying that he'd killed Leslie Cox for the murders, but the townspeople didn't believe him, so they killed him. No one was ever charged in the murder of "Bloody" Ed Watson.

The Everglades is a remote area, and the people who live there are a law unto themselves. It's best to ask no questions and go about your business.

This story left me feeling a bit exposed on this spit of beach, to what Jimmy Buffett describes as "sharks that live on the land." The land sharks scared me more than the alligators. I was hoping that my sailing buddy was just a sailing buddy, not a serial killer in disguise. This was the second story of a gruesome murder he had told in as many evenings.

I erected my mosquito net and spread my sheet out on the deck pads, making sure that my flare gun was handy in case I had an emergency during the night.

A flare gun is a very important piece of safety equipment, and mine, which looked like a large orange pistol, was top-of-the-line from ACR. When you have a life-threatening problem at sea, you load a flare into the muzzle and shoot it up into the air. Someone sees the flare and will alert the authorities. You then continue to shoot up flares at intervals until you run out of flares, are rescued, or drown.

The gun could do serious damage to a land shark at close range, so I kept it handy.

It was actually a wonderful night under my mosquito netting, with the cool breezes and a view of the stars. This was the way to camp. The weather was getting warm enough not to have to bother with that pesky sleeping bag. My sheet was enough. I was a little damp with the morning dew, but the sun quickly took care of that problem. The best part of the night was when I didn't wake up dead.

***

The morning brought calm seas and very little breeze. We took advantage of what little morning breeze there was, and then had to go under power. I noticed Steve hesitating at what looked to me to be the mouth of a channel. My GPS clearly had it marked as the entrance of the Shark River. I sailed up to Steve as he was taking bearings with his handheld compass.

I asked if he wanted to do it the old-fashioned way or would follow me into the 21st century of the GPS. He said lead on, and we motored into the mouth of the Shark River to get to Whitewater Bay on the eastern end of the Waterway. We chose to go down the Joe River side of the bay, as it was sheltered and had minimal boat traffic. There were wonderful Tiki shelters built next to the mangroves, with Porta-Potties. We stopped at one shelter for lunch.

As we got close to Buttonwood Canal, we started getting into the fishing and tourist traffic. This was to be our final leg to Flamingo. As we moved down the canal, I noticed a bridge. I kept looking for the bridge tender's house and trying to figure out how to get them to raise the bridge so I could go under it. I then noticed Steve easily removing his unstayed masts and putting them in the bottom of his boat.

It slowly dawned on me that there was no bridge tender and I would either have to drop my mast or turn around and do the 50-some miles on the outside to Flamingo. Out came the tools. Of course, they were buried under a tent and a sleeping bag. It was very awkward trying to get the boat and me ready for the job. The canal was very narrow and there was lots of boat traffic.

Steve motored over to me and we tied the boats together. I was then able to put all my concentration into unhooking the stays and lowering and stowing the 20-foot mast and sail onto the deck. It took me about 20 minutes in real time, but felt like forever in that narrow canal.

This was one of the dangers of sailing with another person. I had depended on his knowledge of the area, but he didn't know about my boat. I should have looked at the charts, but I'd gotten lazy because I had an escort. It could have been a really bad situation if I hadn't been able to lower the mast and get under the bridge. I didn't have enough provisions for several more days of sailing.

It would have been difficult fighting the current, using the little fuel I had left to make the 50-mile trip back around the outside edge of the Everglades. I learned my lesson, not to be dependent on others' knowledge but to do the research myself. Only I knew my boat's capabilities.

We pulled into Flamingo as it was getting dark and found slips for the boats. Since the boats both had masts on the deck, it would be impossible to sleep on them. The park had a hotel, and there were two rooms available. We paid to sleep in nice beds, have air conditioning, and be able to take a hot, freshwater shower in the morning. We also had a nice meal at the park restaurant.

Steve was packing up to go home, and I was trying to decide whether to follow the Intracoastal south to Marathon or go due east to Key Largo. Going to Marathon would take several more days. I wanted to go due east, but there were very few charts of this route and it wasn't well marked. I could end up like the pygmies my guru had described, lost in the mangroves in a crocodile sanctuary.

There was a strong front coming in, so I didn't have to make a decision immediately. My next obstacle was the dyke. I knew that there was a dyke at the end of Buttonwood canal, separating it from Florida Bay. There was a big sign on the dyke lift that said no boats under 14 feet could be lifted over. Once again, I was a victim of my own lack of research.

I approached the park rangers, looking for another way around. They said that they had a ramp on the other side of the dyke where boats could be launched. We put our heads together and they offered to get a truck and trailer and tow my boat around the dyke. This was easily accomplished because the mast was already down.

***

The next morning, I said goodbye to Steve and thanked him for his company and his knowledge of the Ten Thousand Islands. I put my boat back together around feeding time for the local mosquitoes. The homemade nontoxic repellent I had packed apparently encouraged them. I was bloody by the time I finished putting up the mast.

I took a break in the convenience store and called Bobbi to check in. I'd had a request for a phone interview with the *St. Petersburg Times* and put in the call. I also wrote up and mailed my report of my trip from Naples to Flamingo. I bought a bumper sticker for my boat which read "I gave blood in Flamingo" with a huge mosquito printed on it.

A couple of old fishermen came in to buy supplies. I overhead them talking about going into the backcountry. I asked them about the backcountry and going due east to Key Largo, instead of taking the Intracoastal through Marathon, and then following the Keys north. They said that they made the run between Key Largo and Flamingo on a regular basis and that the channel was marked with PVC pipe.

We pulled a chart off of the shelf and they started going over it with me. They dug out their charts and marked all the compass headings for me through the mangroves.

Just keep heading east. You'll get there.

They gave me the confidence to try it.

I stocked up on food and fuel, but still had enough water to last me a month. I went to sleep early under my mosquito netting, got up with the sun, and quietly motored out of the channel, then raised my sails and turned into the dawn. The water was sparkling in the morning light and all was right with the world.

I saw my first PVC pipe as I approached a small mangrove island. The pipe was pointing to stay to port, and so I did. Lining up the compass, spotting pipes, and enjoying the scenery took up most of my time. There was one spot the fishermen had warned me about, Haulover Canal. They said that I might have to get out and push. They were correct.

Deep in crocodile-infested waters, I jumped out of my boat and pushed it through the canal. The crocs must have been taking a nap; there were none to be seen.

As the sun made its transit west, I continued my journey east. The beauty of this place was amazing. The crystal clear blue water and the green mangroves were pristine, with no evidence of human trash; it was awe-inspiring. My boat quietly sailed along, pushing a bow wake as it danced its way across the bay. The only sounds were the birds, water, and breeze. I had never been in such quiet. There was no hum of the city, jet skis, or powerboats to mask its music.

My final approach into Key Largo was across Blackwater Sound. There was a small opening in the mangroves, right where the fishermen had said it would be. As the afternoon sea breeze freshened, I shot through the pass into the sound.

The water penned on all sides was starting to stack up into a nice chop. The wind continued to build. My nice quiet sail was coming to a screeching climax. I officially surfed my way into the East Coast of Florida.

At the dock, I secured my vessel and made my way to the Tiki bar. I'd survived the Glades and had never seen any of those "Wheretheheckrwee" pygmy Indians or crocodiles. It was time to share my tale over a piña colada in Key Largo.

The cruising crowd and the regulars were just toasting the sunset when I strolled up.

"What boat did you come in on?" they asked.

"The *Prevail*," I said proudly.

"You know, it gets real rough in the bay; I bet the marina could set you up for the night."

"They did. My vessel is over there at the dock," I replied as it was beginning to dawn on them that the *Prevail* was what they were looking at.

"You sailed in on that?"

"Yes," I replied

"Where do you hail from?"

"St. Petersburg, Florida"

"Where did you sail from?"

"Made the run from Flamingo to here today. Been cruising now for a couple of weeks."

"I know who you are," said a guy at the end of the bar with a gray ponytail and a rum drink. "You're the cancer survivor sailing to Maine in the dinghy."

"Yes," I replied.

"I'm Jerry, captain of the motorsailer *Southwinds*. I'm a retired veteran with a disability. I've been following your trip. Let's have a look at your vessel."

The group took a respite from the rum and made their way over to the dock. I gave them the tour. It didn't last long enough for the ice in their drinks to melt.

One of the cruisers told me about a Bermuda high that was pumping a heavy breeze up the East Coast. The weatherman called for 20-25 knot winds for the next week and four-foot seas. Their plan was to wait it out tucked snugly into Key Largo. Coming off the high of my Flamingo-Key Largo run, bolstered by the courage of rum, I replied that I had to start up the East Coast tomorrow. I had a date to keep in Miami.

They suggested that I stay inside and keep close to shore. Sailors call being on the ocean "outside"; the Intracoastal is the "inside." We looked at some possible bailout places if the weather got too dicey. Jerry told me he would email my family and Bobbi and let them know that I'd made it safely to Key Largo. Sailors are the best people in the world!

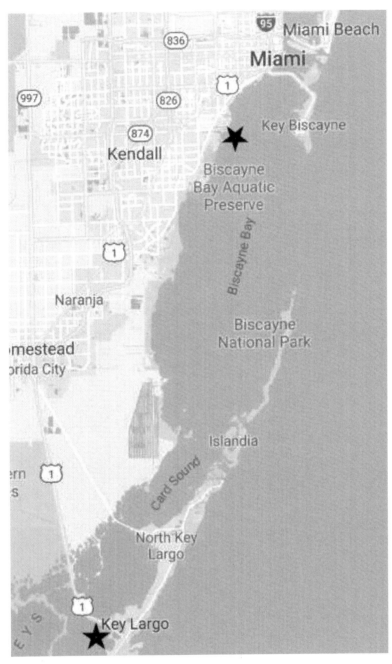

Key Largo, FL to Miami, FL

CHAPTER 12

Forget safety.
Live where you fear to live.
Destroy your reputation.
Be notorious.

~

- Rumi -

Key Largo, Florida to Miami, Florida
April 26 to April 27, 2000

Early the next morning, I carried the gas tanks over to the gas station and topped them off for the Miami run. It was about 50 miles, the longest I had attempted in one day. I could stop in the bay along the way if I needed to and anchor for the night.

I really loved those nights at anchor in the wilds. When I was at a marina, I put up the tent for privacy, as I really didn't want anyone watching me sleep. But when I was out in the wilderness at anchor, I put up the mosquito netting and allowed the boat to gently rock me to sleep. There was no one to disturb my rest.

Everything shipshape, I pulled out of the slip and approached the drawbridge at US-1, the highway I would parallel all the way to Maine. US-1 starts in Key West and runs 2,377 miles to Kent, Maine. I was beginning to feel like a real sailor. I'd left the West Coast of Florida, my water playground. It was time to take on the Atlantic.

The waters from Miami to Key Largo were also familiar. I had spent many a day windsurfing across Biscayne Bay and snorkeling off Cutler

113

Ridge looking for lobster. Now, I was headed to Shake-a-Leg Miami. Shake-a-Leg, founded by Harry Horgan, had grown to be a premiere sailing venue for people with disabilities.

The bridge tender honked, stopped the traffic, and opened the bridge for me to pass into Barnes Sound. Barnes Sound is the body of water between Key Largo and Card Sound. It's a shallow sound with the dredged Intracoastal Waterway running up through the middle. Motorists have to pay $1.00 to cross this gateway to the Keys. We sailors get to use the waterways for free.

I was the only vessel on this section of the Intracoastal as I motored through the mangrove canal on my approach to the sound. Barnes and Card Sound were home to many people who came to live the simple life that the sea provided. On the north end there was a canal and an awesome restaurant, Alabama Jack's, that had the best crab cakes in the world. I thought I might just stop there for the night, if the weather put up a stink.

I had donned my foul weather gear before leaving the dock. Gill had provided me with two tops, a breeze breaker, a full foul weather jacket with hood, and foul weather pants. They also provided boots to keep my feet warm once I got further north. I had my lifejacket and knife where I could easily reach them, having heard of sailors in full foul weather gear being pulled to the bottom of the ocean by the sheer weight of their clothes. A knife to cut myself free of any encumbrance was a necessity.

As I left the mangroves, I could see the wind on the water. Two- to four-foot waves looked about right, and the confused morning breeze was fighting the high. Of course, I was headed right into it! As I passed the channel marker, a wave broke over my bow and I knew I was in for a rough ride. I turned my boat so that I took the waves on a 45-degree angle and headed toward the western shore of the bay. Maybe I could get into smoother water, and if I had enough of being beaten up sailing, I could get out and walk!

As the sun heated up, the land breeze settled a little bit. I continued to make my way up the western shore; at this pace, I might reach Miami by next month. I finally got into the lee of the land just before the Card Sound Bridge. I anchored in the smooth water to warm up in the sun and chew on a power bar. Should I stop or should I go on?

I had made up a lot of time by sailing across Florida Bay instead of staying in the channel of the Intracoastal Waterway, so I could stop and rest. It was tempting. The waves and wind had dropped and I expected the afternoon sea breeze to come in and push me on north to Miami. I was also really feeling the need to see some familiar faces and sleep in a real bed.

This was not the first or the last time I was going to have to make the decision to proceed or rest. Miami was so close, it was calling my name. I raised the sail, weighed the anchor, and headed under the bridge into Little Card Sound, passing up those crab cakes. But I would return.

It was 2:00 in the afternoon when I sighted the stacks at Turkey Point power plant. By this time, I was having a lovely sail up the bay. I'd been able to cut down on distance to be sailed as I didn't have to stay in the channel—the advantages of a shallow draft. I was officially in Biscayne Bay. Since I'd gone to graduate school in Miami, it felt like I was coming home. I was going to see Shawn, and the anticipation of reaching Miami overrode any exhaustion I might have felt.

The waves had settled, the sun was warm, and the wind was fresh. I decided to head on up the bay and see how close I could get to Shake-a-Leg in Coconut Grove before dark. I checked my cell phone and tried to put in a call to my friend Allen Fiske, who lived aboard at Shake-a-Leg. I wasn't in range. I tried the VHF handheld radio and again, I wasn't in range. So, I pulled an apple out of my provisions and happily crunched my way up Biscayne Bay.

Allen is one of those incredible people who doesn't let his disability get in the way of a full life. He has paraplegia and lives on a large sailboat he has adapted to meet his needs. He also has a Coast Guard captain's license and takes people out sailing on Biscayne Bay. He knows these waters like the back of his hand and has no time for sissies.

Black Point was the next landmark. It would be a race to the dock. Would I beat the sun? The insurance company didn't allow me to sail after dark. I was starting to push that envelope. On up past Cutler Ridge, I'd spent a lovely day back in my youth being dragged behind a fishing boat looking for lobster just off of this spit of land. I could see some of the coral heads and wondered if there was a tasty meal hiding underneath one.

Next, was Matheson Hammock Park, and another call to Shake-a-

Leg. Allen picked up on the first ring and asked my position. He said I would see the marker flashing green at Dinner Key channel if night fell before I got there. He would get a powerboat to come out and guide me in from there.

As I approached the Dinner Key light in the dusk, I heard a cheer go up from the land. Could they see me coming? Had Allen called everyone and let them know I was coming in? I was overwhelmed with excitement and anticipation. I knew that the sponsors were going to hold a party and press conference for me in Miami, but Allen was the only one who knew that I was coming in. Maybe my gray-haired ponytailed Key Largo friend had sent the message north from the Keys. Email was definitely faster than my boat!

Allen had enlisted the help of Fred, one of the staff members at Shake-a-Leg; they came out in a powerboat to meet me at the head of the channel and escorted me to the dock. All was quiet and there was no one there. Had I imagined the cheer? Have I been at sea too long? This had been my longest day on the water, but I wasn't sure it would qualify for hallucinations. How did I ask about the cheering without sounding like an egotistical fool?

Curiosity got the better of me and I said nonchalantly that I'd heard a cheer go up as I approached the channel. "What's up?"

"Oh, you've been gone a while. You know who Elián González is?"

"No."

"He's a young boy from Cuba and there's a dispute going on over whether he should be sent back home or stay here in the U.S. There was a meeting at City Hall here in Coral Gables, that's where the cheering was coming from; they just fired the city commissioner."

"Oh," I replied. *That isn't my concern; I have to concentrate on docking and doing my job,* I thought. Little did I know the impact that this incident would have on my life.

What a wonderful homecoming Miami was. The sponsors decided not to have the party in Miami and delayed it until Ft. Lauderdale. This was because of all the unrest caused by contention among family, country, and a young man named Elián.

Lisa Wallace and Lesa Wiekel had come over from Clearwater. Lisa Wallace has paraplegia and was involved in the community sailing

116

program with SPPD. Lesa Weikel had a job doing public relations for a local charity. They were both assisting with the media contacts and communication for the Prevail trip.

Shake-a-Leg treated me like a queen, helping me get my boat fixed up, the bottom cleaned, and posting the American flag on the backstay. Shawn took possession of my stove, canned food, sleeping bag, used charts, and everything else I had determined I didn't need. I bought a vinyl tablecloth backed with flannel to use as a blanket and moisture deterrent. It would suffice. We went out to dinner with friends, and I just rested.

I did get to talk to a group of young sailors with spina bifida at Shake-a-Leg. The courage of these children gave me the nerve to keep moving forward. I also heard from a class of children in China. My cousin taught at the International School in Beijing, and their students were following the trip as part of their geography lessons. Closer to home, a school group in Melrose, Florida was also following the trip. They planned on a field trip to meet me when I reached St. Augustine.

I loved reading the emails from the school children Lisa had brought with her. They wanted to know all sorts of things: what kind of sea creatures I saw, how I went to the bathroom, what I ate, what I did during storms, and did I get sea sick? I was looking forward to talking to the Melrose class. I sent back a few answers for Lisa to post on the website.

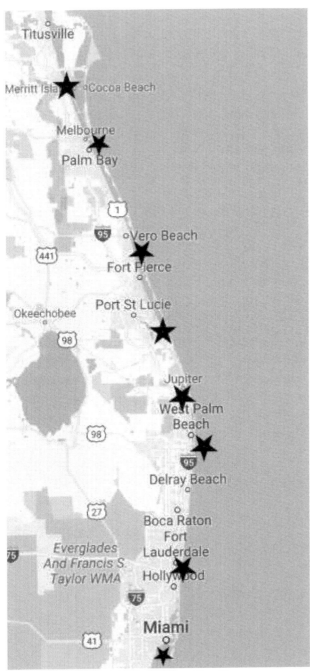

Miami, FL to Titusville, FL

CHAPTER 13

Trouble creates a capacity to handle it.

~

- Oliver Wendell Holmes -

Miami, Florida to Titusville, Florida
April 27 to May 9, 2000

It was time to head north to Ft. Lauderdale. The big question was— inside or out? It was still windy, and the Atlantic was full of waves. I couldn't get out through the channel, up to Ft. Lauderdale, and back inside before dark. So, I would run the Intracoastal.

The staff at Shake-a-Leg followed me out of Dinner Key channel and up the Intracoastal to the Venetian Isles Bridge, just opposite the Port of Miami. They waved goodbye, and I continued my way north. Since it was a weekday, the boat traffic was minimal. It was strange sailing through a city after I had spent a week in the Ten Thousand Islands.

As the day wore on, the Intracoastal narrowed and became more congested. A couple of kids on jet skis came zooming over to me and started cutting donuts, throwing water into my boat. I tried to wave them off, as I couldn't outrun them. They started laughing. Soon, a powerboat flying an upside down American flag approached. This was the solidarity symbol being used by the Cubans as protest of the Elián González issue. It looked to be the "responsible" adults who were overseeing the kids on the jet-ski, but they joined in the fun of trying to swamp me. Suddenly it dawned on me that I was flying the American flag right-side up. I was seen as a threat.

I grabbed my radio; it was always on channel 16, which is designated as the international distress frequency. Most sailors monitor 16 at all times. It's used not only for emergencies, but to contact another boat. No one responded to my call. With all the buildings close by, the signal might not be strong enough. I quickly got on the phone to ask for help. I called Tom Casey with *Sail Magazine*, who would be meeting me in Ft. Lauderdale. He got my position and said he would alert the marine patrol. I just kept slowly motoring north, feeling so helpless. All I could do was keep bailing and sailing. Eventually, they tired of the game and zoomed off. The marine patrol never showed up.

After they left, I entered a section of the Intracoastal I dubbed "the canyon." There were huge condos, restaurants, and businesses built up right to the edge of the water. Any wake coming off the back of a boat hit the solid concrete wall and bounced back and forth across the waterway, until it wore itself out or another wave overcame it. It was a bit like motoring through a washing machine on agitate. *Agitate* was also a good word to describe my mood!

I was beat when I pulled into the marina at Cabo Rico Yachts. The PR people for SIMRAD and ACR met me at the dock. They saw my state of mind and said they were having a hard time getting publicity because of the Elián González issue. I shook my head and told them my story of the jet skis and not being able to get any help as I was being tormented. I understood people wanting to stand up for their beliefs. I, too, was an activist, but I drew the line at doing harm to others and their property.

I wanted to be treated with respect, and I treated others with respect, even if we had differences. It's the differences that make us stronger.

The PR people made a couple of calls and the press inundated me. They wanted to know about the jet ski attack, so I told them my story. I talked about the need for training, respect, and laws needed for jet ski users, as well as the wonderful support I was getting from the sponsors. They left to get their stories in, and I got a shower and dinner. We had a small sponsor party. Ken from SPPD had driven over from Sarasota to check on things. He joined us, but didn't have any more cash for me. I was still on my own financially.

Next to my slip on the dock was a nice-looking gentleman with an even nicer looking Cabo Rico sailboat. He was there getting an overhaul;

well, the boat was getting an overhaul. He was from Seattle, Washington, and was getting ready to sail it home. I was ready to sign on as crew. He invited me to join him for coffee the next morning before I left the dock, a wonderful invitation, and a nice ending to a tough day.

So much for daydreams of the Caribbean and sunsets on a Cabo! The coffee was tasty and the company was good, but it was time to head north toward West Palm Beach. I had spent several years working and living in West Palm, so it was another homecoming. The Intracoastal led up through apartment complexes; as I was going by, people were out on their balconies with their newspapers shouting *"Prevail!"* It was incredible. I felt like royalty, smiling and waving. The morning news had published the story. The support was overwhelming.

Having ridden jet skis, I knew it was a blast, and also very easy to forget when you were having so much fun that your actions could negatively impact others. The rule of the sea is to take care of each other, watch each other's backs, and do no harm. Also, to offer to rescue people who are in trouble, because one day you might need to be rescued. It was nice to feel the support. I had struck a chord; many people were concerned about the safety of our waterways and our fellow man.

***

I was able to make it into Lake Worth as it was getting dark. I needed a place to stay, but I didn't have one scheduled. I remembered Dr. Kelly, the psychiatrist I'd worked for who had been so supportive when I lost my eye, had a mansion on Palm Beach. I had been to his dock several times when I worked for him. I remembered there was no floating dock and it would not be easy to tie to, but any dock was looking good!

I got just north of the pass and turned into his dock. The tide was out, pilings were available to tie to, but I wasn't sure I could climb up to the dock. I called my old roommate, DeDe, and let her know I had arrived. She said she would come out and visit me.

Finally figuring out a way to climb up the pilings, I pulled myself onto the dock. The house was dark; I guessed Dr. Kelly wasn't home. I started to walk around the estate and see if I could find anyone.

He has a widow's walk on top of the house, where I had spent several Fourth of Julys watching the fireworks up and down the coast. The last time I'd seen him, he had also had a huge mastiff, so I was treading carefully. I started to notice construction barriers, and realized the house was vacant. He had moved and no one was home. I guessed I could still make use of the dock for the night. I went back to the dock and made the six-foot climb back down to my deck.

It was getting dark and was time to settle in for the night. I'd just finished putting up the mosquito netting when I heard a small voice calling. It was DeDe. "Down here!" I cried. I put the light on myself and she made the climb down the pilings to the boat.

"How did you get in?" I asked.

She said she'd jumped the fence and had also met the new owner, who'd told her I could stay the night at the dock. I broke out the spare peanut M&M's and water. We had a great evening, talking over old times.

The next morning, I sailed up Lake Worth. I had owned a 29-foot Columbia, the boat I sold to the man with lung cancer, and these were my old sailing grounds. Things had changed in the ten years that I had been away. There was much more big boat traffic. I got a real taste of boat wakes.

I had a date with a harbor pilot and his family up on the north end of the lake before the Intracoastal narrowed again. My friend Jorge had set me up with this berth. He had solicited the support of all the harbor pilots up and down the East Coast of the U.S. Once again, I found myself at the bottom of a huge dock. This time, there was a concrete wall. Climbing was another skill I was starting to add to my résumé. The docks were so high in this area for two reasons: first, the tides, and second, the hurricanes. It worked for a boat of regular size, but for *Prevail*, not so well!

I was glad to have a safe place to tie up the boat so I could go and meet my friends for dinner and shopping. It was great. Though I hadn't seen them in several years, it was like no time had passed at all; we just picked up where we left off.

When I got back to the boat, I erected the mosquito net. I put some dryer sheets in the rigging close to the netting, having been told this would keep the mosquitoes away. It worked! I started calling it my "mosquito voodoo."

The next morning, I took off for points north, not sure how far I was going to go that day. I was still in somewhat familiar territory, making my way north toward Jupiter. Once past the inlet and the famous lighthouse, I broke out of the constraining Intracoastal into Hobe Sound. I was astounded; Hobe Sound sparkled like an emerald. The change in the color of the water and the clarity made my day.

I decided it was a great place to pull up the sail, break out a little lunch, and sail slowly across the sound drinking in the beauty of the area. The sail was too brief when, once again, the waterway narrowed past the St. Lucie Inlet and I started looking for a place to spend the night.

Once past the inlet, I had to go under another bridge that my mast easily cleared. I turned east toward the barrier island and causeway and anchored off of a beach with a tent on it which read, "U.S. Sailing School of Martin County." I took advantage of the shallow water and scrubbed the growth off the bottom of the boat. The last time this had been done was in Miami. No antifouling paint had been put on the boat, and it was amazing how quickly the seaweed can grow and foul up the bottom. It was nasty.

Feeling quite the self-sufficient sailor, I got out an apple and a granola bar and had dinner. As usual, I stuffed a tea bag into a bottle of water to infuse overnight for breakfast. I set up mosquito netting and voodoo, cuddled under my tablecloth, and settled in for a wonderful night's sleep.

The next morning, I headed toward Vero Beach. The name of this stretch of the Intracoastal was the Indian River. It was wide enough to sail, and sail I did. Even though this slowed my progress, it was much more enjoyable than motoring. That evening I enjoyed time with a wonderful couple from Vero Beach Yacht Club who had offered me a slip and dinner for the night. Another couple at the yacht club provided breakfast. Things were definitely looking up on my meager budget. The angels of the Intracoastal would provide. After breakfast, I motored out into the Intracoastal, set my sails, and headed north. I was on my way to Melbourne.

I was born at Camp Lejeune, North Carolina. My father and a fellow dental officer had become fast friends during his tour of duty there. His wife and my mom were pregnant at the same time. They had a son, Mark, and mom had me. The son and I were cradle mates. As Navy life went, duty stations separated them, but their friendship continued. Now retired, Dr. Enoch had arranged for me to keep the boat at Eau Galle Yacht Club. There was a good hot shower, a hot meal, and a clean bed waiting for me. It was another wonderful homecoming. Dr. Enoch also made sure I was well provisioned for the next leg of the trip.

The next morning, I was off sailing to Titusville. The weather was perfect, with a nice breeze and a wonderful wide river for sailing. The boat was handling great, but I still had some trepidation. The worst part of the sail was the boat traffic. I liked it when I could get out of the channel and sail in open water.

As the day wore on, I checked in with the weather channel. They were reporting a front on its way south, with storms due to hit Titusville in the afternoon. I knew I had to get under the bridge in Titusville before rush hour. This was the commuting bridge out the Cape Canaveral. They didn't open this bridge to boat traffic when everyone was driving home, and there were a lot of people who worked at NASA.

I stopped for lunch to take a break and to check on the weather again. Titusville was currently receiving golf ball-sized hail. I had noticed the wind was coming up and whitecaps were forming on the river, so I decided to drop the main and start the engine. I had to make the last bridge opening.

I was motorsailing under jib running toward Titusville, dodging storms and boat traffic. Then I stopped the engine to gas up and the engine wouldn't restart. The jib gave me enough steerage to keep me out of harm's way. I pulled the cord desperately until my arm ached. It was to no avail.

I noticed another storm coming straight at me. I needed to pass under a bridge to get to the next marina and safety. It was dangerous being on the water in a lightning storm in a small boat with no cover, and now I had no engine. I had to decide whether or not to raise the mainsail. With the wind continuing to strengthen and the skies getting dark, the main would increase my speed north to safety, and increase the likelihood of being capsized.

I saw another squall coming across the water to the south. It was amazing to see the rain disturbing the surface of the water, coming toward you, gray and menacing. I looked for a place to shelter, a small island to hide behind. The squall didn't reach me; it stayed south as I moved north.

I knew that I wasn't going to be so lucky next time. I decided to raise the main sail and put a reef in it, thereby making it smaller. This would give me a little more speed and steerage, but not overwhelm the boat. Using full sail in conditions of high winds is just asking to be capsized. I had previous experience sailing upside down in my racing days, and I was not interested in repeating it.

The speed I was making under reefed sail was not enough to make it to the marina at Titusville before the worst of the storms arrived. I decided to make a run for the shore instead and see if I could find a place to pull in. I could see the stacks of a power plant rising on the shore; maybe they had some docks, and some people to help, I thought hopefully. They would make a great landmark to navigate to when the rain blocked most my vision. I set the helm toward the power plant.

Another squall came across the water and I started to be pelted by rain and hail. Lightning crackled all around me. Sitting soaking wet under a great big lightning rod, I had to be careful not to touch any metal. I pulled out my jumper cables and attached one end to the shroud and the other, I let dangle in the water. This should divert any electricity and ground it to the water, not to me!

I had on my foul weather jacket and a lifejacket. I was much better prepared now for bad weather than at the beginning of the trip. I got to the breakwater of the power plant and as I was rounding it, looking for a safe anchorage, I saw the dock.

It was so inviting. There were white bumpers along the edge of the floating dock to protect the boats, a Tiki hut with a picnic table, mobile homes, and a flag flapping on a pole. I sailed to the dock and came alongside, just as another squall passed to the north on its way to the sea. Making the boat fast, I quickly took the cover off the engine to effect a repair. I made ready to seek cover in the Tiki hut, in case the storms made another direct hit.

Several elderly women came out of their trailers and made their way down to the dock. I asked them if I could stay there long enough to fix my engine, hoping they would provide shelter from the storm.

The reply came, "We don't know anything about sailboats."

Pleading my case, I told them I didn't expect them to fix my engine, I just needed a safe harbor. Once again came the reply. "We don't know anything about sailboats."

I figured I must look like an alien landed from a strange world. A woman all alone in a small dinghy, wearing foul weather gear over an oversized long-sleeve white shirt, pink pajama bottoms, and a floppy hat. They did live across the river from Cape Canaveral; I might not have been the first odd creature to land unannounced at their door.

A man came quietly down to the dock and a look of relief spread across the faces of the women. They immediately fell back to make room for him. The lines on his face portrayed his wisdom. He introduced himself as Dan and asked if he could help. I explained the problem I was having with the engine.

Dan smiled and with that quiet confidence, said, "Let me take a look." With relief, I turned the outboard over to his more experienced hands. The women, forgetting the words to their chorus, broke into small groups and gossiped their way back to their trailers. It was starting to rain again.

Dan told me I had landed in South Titusville. He asked me if I had been invited into a home. I shook my head no and said that I was hoping to be allowed to stand under the Tiki hut until the storm passed. He smiled and said that I would be standing for a long time, as the storms were supposed to continue all night. He invited me to stay in his in-laws' trailer, as they had gone north for the summer. He told me that he would fix the engine, and that I was to go up to his trailer and his wife would give me a hot meal. Tears of gratitude sprang to my eyes.

I made my way up the street and he followed behind me with the carburetor from the engine. He brought along my almost-empty gas can to refill.

The beef stew we had was the best I'd ever tasted. After dinner, we drove into town and he bought the necessary items to get me going again. And it continued to rain.

Dan had been the supervisor of maintenance for a local company, and was forced into early retirement due to a near-fatal heart attack. The attack left him with half a heart. He and his wife lived simply. His great joy was in fixing and creating things to make the world a better place. He was currently working on a machine to clean and revitalize ponds. He had earned the title "the Inventor."

That night, at their insistence, I slept in a warm, dry bed, safe from the storms which raged all night.

The next morning, I bailed out the boat while he fixed my engine. I left the dock, with him and his dog wishing me a safe journey. I made the bridge opening and headed north, watching for a sharp right turn to take me into Mosquito Lagoon. This body of water was part of the Canaveral National Seashore and the Indian River.

The sharp right turn was known as Haulover Canal. I got there about noon. As I motored through the narrow waterway, I heard the barking of a dog. I looked up to see the Inventor smiling and waving from the shore. I gave him the thumbs up on the engine and he returned the same.

Half a heart ... I would argue otherwise.

Titusville, FL to Jacksonville, FL

CHAPTER 14

Adopt the pace of nature; her secret is patience.

~

- Ralph Waldo Emerson -

Titusville, Florida to Jacksonville, Florida
May 9 to May 19, 2000

The storms had put me behind and I was not going to make it to Daytona Beach on time, so I consulted my charts and noticed New Smyrna Beach Yacht Club. I could pull in there and ask for dockage for the night. Raising the yacht club on my radio, I requested and was given permission to dock. I asked for a dinghy dock, but the dock master did not quite understand why. Instead, he sent me to an empty slip. I was learning about the tides in these parts and made sure my lines had plenty of stretch. The commodore was a woman and invited me to dinner, saying I could use the showers first!

She plied me with a couple of margaritas and I happily made my way back to *Prevail*. Just as I had expected, the tide had gone out and I had a long jump to the deck. I put up my mosquito netting and voodoo. Being in a place called Mosquito Lagoon, I felt it was the right thing to do.

***

The next morning, I headed to Daytona Yacht Club, but first I had to make my way through the Aquatic Preserve of Mosquito Lagoon. This area had been fished out several decades before and commercial net fishing was disallowed.

As a result, the residents of this area discovered that it was the perfect place to raise clams. Clams are very good to eat and very good for the environment. People were out working their clam farms as I sailed by.

The Halifax River Yacht Club on Daytona Beach had gotten the message that I had been delayed by the storms and had rearranged its schedule. Jim Myers and his wife Susan met me at the dock. They had driven over from St. Pete Beach to provide some emotional support and take me out to lunch.

I was interviewed by the Daytona Beach newspaper and did a live television interview by phone with Channel 10 in Tampa Bay. The good folks at the Yacht Club threw a party in my honor and the mayor recognized my accomplishment. They also checked out my engine and made sure I had plenty of fuel for the trip north.

It wasn't all about me. The manager of the yacht club was facing cancer, and we spent time talking about the things I had done to heal. We got into the spiritual and emotional issues surrounding a cancer diagnosis, which was very healing for both of us. As I made my way to a Beneteau 51, where I had been offered a berth for the night, a feeling of warmth came over me. I noticed the name of the boat in the slip next to mine, *Hallelujah!*

We're all struggling in this world. The trip had been a struggle and triumph at the same time. Life's journey is that way, stopping to celebrate each success and move through each trial, adjusting our sails. Hallelujah!

Next stop was St. Augustine, where the *Prevail* was built; Chris Bauer had his shop and home there. Ken and his wife Jill were on their way to meet me and assist with boat maintenance. This was to be a three-day stop to clean the bottom of the boat, paint it, and give it an overhaul before I headed north. My parents drove over from Melrose to see me. I also had a visit from the fifth-grade elementary class who had been following the trip online. It was so much fun spending time with the kids. They were so curious. It was a great exchange.

I left St. Augustine three days later, rejuvenated, with the boat in tip-top condition. I was on the radio when a familiar voice broke in. It was Cindy from St. Petersburg. Cindy and Al are yacht surveyors. When someone goes to purchase a used yacht, they want it surveyed, just like a home inspection. You want to make sure you know exactly what you're getting.

They tried to catch up with me in Palm Valley, but I already had plans for dinner with some new friends, Ed and Priscilla. Ed, a wonderful chef, cooked us dinner. Ed also was what I called "plugged in." He would get spiritual inspirations to share with people. He suddenly looked at me and said, "You really don't understand what you're doing yet and why, but in two to three years, you will understand."

There are some people who have the gift of knowing, and I take this sharing very seriously.

Priscilla took me to her friend Nancy's house to spend the night. Nancy was a massage therapist and did a technique called zero balancing, which relieves tension and pain, improves balance, and quiets the mind. I really needed that mind quieting! After the treatment, I lounged in a bath of Epsom salts, reflecting on the people I had met and the welcoming care I had received at every turn, even when I was scared out of my mind. There is a force, a God, a spirit that moves through all things. It's a matter of belief and trust.

Trust is hard when you're all alone on a tiny boat, at the mercy of the weather and the big powerful boats around you. There's a feeling of helplessness and I was overwhelmed at times with the fear. Chris Bauer's wife shared a story of fear with me about when they were sailing off the coast of Africa in a big storm. They didn't know if they would last the night.

Sometimes I didn't know if I was going to last the next few minutes. I'd see a big cigarette boat bearing down on me with the skipper sipping on a cocktail and would try to stay out of the way, but even my little boat had to stay in the channels sometimes. I really wondered what I was doing, day after day, crawling my way north slower than I could walk.

Al wrote to me later, putting a few things in perspective:

I am always amazed as I stroll piers in marinas that are chock-a-block with large ocean capable vessels that never leave the slip. The owners constantly plan ... and spend ... and equip for the great trip they rarely take. In many cases, the oceangoing vessels are too cumbersome to get away from the pier with shorthanded crew.

I guess those big boats fulfill their mission as "dream machines" and psychological stress reducers for those unlikely to put them to use. Great to encounter someone like you with the guts, ability, and drive to make the leap. You remind us that most limitations are in our heads rather than in our bodies ... or our wallets. Inspirational ... and much appreciated.

I don't know about the guts. To be honest, doing this trip was more about being high profile, I always had people watching me. I am reminded of the rower in the Everglades who was doing his trip in the unknown. Now that took courage. He had no one to answer to and no one would have been the wiser if he'd decided to pack his boat up and go home. He was doing it for himself. I was doing this for others. It would have been so much easier to do this on one of those big boats Al was referring to, with a full crew!

***

The next morning, I left Palm Valley on my way north to Jacksonville. Jacksonville is a huge port city, with lots of commercial shipping. The dock where I was headed was right in the middle of the port. As I passed under the last bridge into the St. John's River, the current became wicked. I was glad to be motorsailing at this point. It felt a bit like I was trying to walk on ice, slipping and sliding in all sorts of directions as the tides of the Atlantic met the Intracoastal Waterway and the St. John's River.

I had waited in the Intracoastal for the tide to be favorable to Blount Island, and I was glad. I could not even imagine bucking this tide.

There were many freighters going in and out of the port, some loaded and headed to parts across the ocean, some coming in to let off their cargo. Many people asked me if I found those huge ships scary. Not really; I actually had tremendous respect for them. The captains of these vessels were highly trained and knew exactly where they had to be in order to have maneuvering room. But I had one big advantage: I could sail where they could not.

As long as I left the deep shipping channels to them and let them go first, then there was no problem. They had to stay in the channel, so I knew where they were going. It was the faster, smaller boats with amateurs partying at the helm that gave me fits.

I made my way by all the freighters at the commercial dock and went around the side of Blount Island. I had called ahead, letting them know my ETA. I was spending the night at a place with a program for teenage boys, called Safe Harbor. The program reminded me of my days working in Dr. Kelly's program. The boys lived there full-time, went to school, and learned marine skills so they would be employable when they finished the program. They had to earn privileges, one of which was getting to take out a sailboat for a weekend.

Several young men met me at the dock. They smartly tied up my boat and took my trash bag and overnight bag. Not only were they being taught marine skills, they were clearly being taught manners!

While I was in Jacksonville, I went to speak to a program for at-risk girls called Girls, Inc. The girls were awesome and had so many wonderful dreams for their futures. They were going to have bright futures because they were getting the help they needed to move past the obstacles in their lives. No one can do it alone.

I sometimes have this fantasy that I'm so self-sufficient, but really I'm part of a huge interdependent network. We're all working together to help each other move past obstacles.

The next morning I was given a tow by one of the staff and one of the boys at Safe Harbor to the entrance of the Intracoastal heading north. The tide was not favorable and without this tow, I would have been tacking back and forth just to stay in one place for hours. As my great uncle used to say, "tide and time wait for no man."

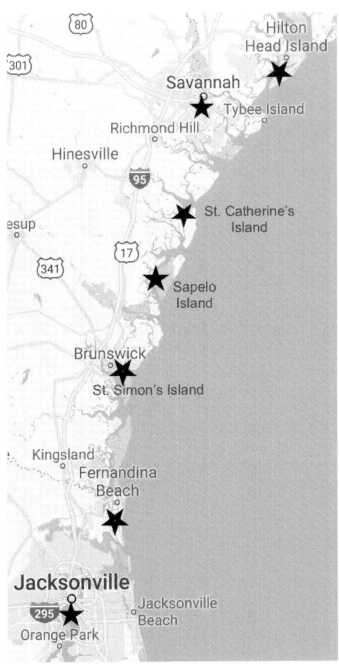

Jacksonville, FL to Hilton Head, SC

CHAPTER 15

Southern Hospitality, Georgia Style

Not a tangible thing, but an attitude which has been ingrained in Southerners forever. It's a feeling of being sincerely welcomed as a guest or a long-lost friend; a way of life that lets people be as warm as the climate. It's an easiness of speaking with total strangers or anyone, a unique friendliness encompassing the whole way of life in the deep south. It is not something one does; it's the way one is.

~

- Anon -

Jacksonville, Florida to Hilton Head, South Carolina
May 19 to May 28, 2000

One more night in my home state and I was finally leaving Florida. A very large state with an even larger coastline, it seemed like I had been sailing forever. The waterway narrowed, and the salt marshes started making an appearance as I headed toward Amelia Island. I had a slip waiting for me at Fernandina Beach. A lovely couple, both great adventurers, were hosting me for the night. It was fun sharing an evening of sea stories with them.

The next morning it was off toward Kings Bay, the U.S. Navy submarine base. I had sailed around submarines before in Charleston Harbor so I knew that even when the deck was above water, there was a lot more boat under water. The result was a sucking of the water toward the hull. So, it was smart to give them plenty of room. I didn't think my little motor could overcome the undertow.

Safely past Kings Bay, the next invisible landmark was the Florida-Georgia line. Now, I was really feeling like I was on an adventure. I was in unfamiliar territory, getting further and further from home. I was overcome with excitement and stood in the cockpit with the tiller between my knees singing "Sweet Georgia Brown" and dancing my way up the Intracoastal toward St. Simon's Island.

I was going to have to cross the mouth of the Satilla River just north of Cumberland Island and then take a narrow waterway, with its many currents, to the west of Jekyll Island that was open to the Atlantic. As I was making my way along Cumberland Island, my chart told me that it was the largest barrier island in the northern hemisphere. It was also a wildlife conservancy and run by the park service. I would love to come back and explore this island sometime.

It was a bit tricky crossing the mouth of the Satilla River as it poured into the Atlantic Ocean. By the time I reached Jekyll Island I was tired, so I stopped for lunch at one of the tourist docks. A boater and tourist haven, Jekyll Island was Georgia's answer to Key West. I just wanted a short break and a bite to eat. After I tied up my boat, I stepped out onto the dock and it felt good to stretch my legs. Sailing long distances can really be a sedentary proposition. It was important to make sure I got enough exercise.

As a sailing buddy pointed out, "the sport of sailing is long periods of boredom interspersed with seconds of panic." I would not go along with the boredom; I was never bored. I loved watching the scenery, navigating the waterway, and figuring out how to overcome the next challenge. But I did agree with the seconds of panic; I'd had more than my share.

A man approached me with a copy of *Soundings Magazine*, saying he'd just been reading the article about my trip, and here I'd pulled up to the dock. He invited me to his trawler for lunch. I continued to be awed by the generosity of people. After lunch, I gave my benefactor a tour of *Prevail*. I then readied the boat to continue my way north and he helped me cast off.

Next, I had a date at St. Simon's Island. Betty was the mother of one of the Sunrise Rotarians from St. Petersburg, Florida. She lived on St. Simon's Island, and her friends Mike and Bonnie made arrangements for me to dock my boat at Golden Isles Marina. That was a bonus, since dockage was starting to come in short supply, as boat captains were migrating from their winter playground in Florida to points north for the summer season.

A captain brought in a 54-foot sport fisherman as I was finishing securing my boat for a two-day stay. He looked at me, looked at my boat, and said, "I want to party with you!"

Sorry, bud, I already have plans. I know about you sailors and a girl in every port.

I just laughed and finished my chores.

Nissan had arranged for a local marine mechanic to take a look at the engine. I was working it hard, and it needed to be properly maintained. I was so grateful to Tom Casey for insisting that I have one. I was equally grateful to Nissan for providing it.

Bonnie and Mike took me to Betty's house, where she had arranged a fish fry. While I was on St. Simon's Island, I spoke to the local Rotary, where I was presented with a $250.00 check for SPPD. I was given a wonderful tour of the island. Betty had the saying at the beginning of this chapter posted on her refrigerator. No truer words were spoken of the reception I received as I made my way up the coast.

I took some time to study the chart and talk to the locals. The next marina was at Kilkenny, 60 miles north, then 30 miles on to Savannah. I had friends waiting for me in Savannah. There was a lot of open water and salt marshes between here and there, so I had to stock up for the trip.

The Intracoastal wound its way through the salt marshes to Doboy Sound. The wind was gusting to 20 knots, but in the sheltered waters of the marshes I was getting the advantage of the breeze without the waves. As I poked the bow of my boat out into the sound, I knew I was in for a rough crossing. I put on my foul weather breeze breaker and life jacket and went forth.

Several hours later, I reached the other side of the sound and got into the shelter of Sapelo Island, looking for an anchorage for the night. There were many creeks that branched off the waterway into the marsh. I found a small one on the chart, not wanting any company out here in the middle of nowhere. I figured I could slip up the shallow creek to anchor and no boats on their way north would run into me in the night.

It was a great plan, and I was grateful for the mosquito netting. The mosquitoes were as hungry in Georgia as they had been in the Keys. I put up my voodoo, ate a meal of peanut butter and apple, and went to sleep.

***

The next morning, I woke with the sun to the barking of the marsh hens. It was so incredible; I was really starting to fall in love with these wild places. As I got back out into the waterway, I noticed the wind was still cranking. I had to cross Sapelo Sound, and it was even bigger than Doboy Sound. The wind and the waves were really going to put me to the test.

I put a reef in the main, geared up, and nosed out into the sound. It was one wild ride, fighting not only the wind and waves, but also the current and the tides coming off the Atlantic Ocean. I was making four knots at times, the fastest the boat had ever gone.

Once safely across the sound and back in the marshes, I threw out the anchor and took a breather. I pulled a granola bar out of my stores to celebrate. It was now only lunchtime and I still had another sound to cross. St. Catherine's was not going to be a piece of cake in this weather, and I wondered if I could get safely across it before dark.

As I weighed anchor, I headed up Blackbeard Creek, which was named after the famous pirate who used to smuggle and pillage up and down this coast. The creek widened out into the sound until I could see the waves. I just could not face a few more hours of fighting, so I turned around and looked for a place to anchor for the night. There was a small creek off to the east of the main creek.

A dolphin took that moment to surface at the entrance of the small creek. It was the sign I needed; I headed that way. As I turned the corner, I saw a floating dock, just my size. There were "no trespassing" signs posted all over it. Sounded like an invitation to me.

I made my way to the dock and tied up. It was then that I noticed a man working on a powerboat with "research vessel" written on the side. He came over to me and asked me my business. I explained about the trip and that I just could not face St. Catherine's Sound this afternoon after having surfed Sapelo Sound this morning. He asked me if I had an escort. I told him I was alone, and he invited me to stay.

St. Catherine's Island has a long and varied history, and was initially inhabited by Native Americans. The Spanish then set up a mission to convert the Guale Indians to Christianity. In 1733, James Oglethorpe founded a colony of morality that was antislavery, anti-strong drink, and anti-lawyer. It changed hands several times, eventually bought by Button Gwinnett, who was a signer of the Declaration of Independence. Then it became a cotton plantation, changing hands several more times before becoming the E.J. Noble Estate, and the Noble Foundation. For a more extensive history on the island, refer to: http://www.stcatherinesisland.org

The Larkin Family, who was in charge of the foundation, decided the best use would be to have a "survival center" that bred endangered species. Zoologists from all over the world came to work on the projects. I got a personal tour of the island and got to hold a baby tortoise, which had been successfully bred on the island. There were lemurs running wild everywhere, gazelles, zebras, and hartebeests; incredible!

I got a tour of the plantation house and was invited to spend the night in one of the converted slave cottages. These cottages were now used to house the visiting scientists. The staff let me use the phone to contact my next stop in Savannah and let them know I was a day behind, but doing fine.

***

The next morning as I emerged from the cabin, an alligator greeted me in the swimming pool. The caretakers gave me a T-shirt and filled up my gas can. I could understand why all the "no trespassing" signs had been posted. This was a very special place that needed to be preserved. I'd been allowed in because I was alone, the weather was threatening, and the good people of St. Catherine's lived by the law of the sea.

The wind was not as bad as it had been yesterday afternoon, and I took off refreshed and ready to meet the challenge of St. Catherine's Sound. As I got ready to nose out into the sound, I noticed my engine was sounding a bit rough. I stopped and put in a new spark plug, not wanting to have problems crossing this big body of water and end up getting swept out into the Atlantic Ocean. I hoisted the sails and was able to get across the sound before the wind and waves got bad.

As I was entering St. Catherine's Sound, a helicopter came in low and buzzed me. I wondered if they were from St. Catherine's Island, making sure I was keeping to my promise and heading north up the Intracoastal to the Ogeechee River and Sound.

Once across the sound, the Intracoastal narrowed and there was a little passageway from the Ogeechee River to the Little Ogeechee River called Hell's Gate. It earned its name because of the currents, and I was going to hit it right with the tide pushing me through.

I noticed a big white ship in the waterway pointed toward Hell's Gate. Not wanting to share the space, I tried to raise her on the radio. It was hard to tell if she was moving or standing still; perceptions can be distorted on the water. As I came along beside her, I noticed she was standing still and had finally answered my hail.

She was not going through the gate, so that cleared me ahead. She asked me where I was. I explained that I was the little sailing dinghy off her port bow. I saw a man lean out of the window on the bridge high above the deck and wave. He said, "I thought you were a buoy on my radar."

I knew I moved slow, but didn't think I was moving slow enough to be seen as standing still! I was thankful my radar reflector was functional and could be seen.

I waved and moved on ahead toward Hell's Gate, taking the first right into the Moon River. It's amazing how stale one can feel after hours on a boat, so I had gotten into the habit of stripping down to my swimsuit and airing myself out for a few minutes every day. Standing at the helm in my swimsuit, I started to sing Mancini's "Moon River" from *Breakfast at Tiffany's* at the top of my lungs. There was not another vessel in sight, thank goodness.

But, as luck would have it, the helicopter reappeared and again swooped down on me. I grabbed my shirt and quickly put it on. A girl does have to have some modesty.

The helicopter moved in front of me and dropped down just off the bow of my boat. The passenger dropped a little red cooler in the water, took pictures, and waved goodbye. I reached out and picked up the cooler as it came alongside. That was some pretty fancy flying.

The copter took off for parts unknown and I opened the cooler with trepidation. It was full of ice water, crackers, and mosquito control stickers. Ice water, wow, what a treat from an unknown benefactor!

The Moon River turned into the Skidaway River as the afternoon storm clouds started gathering. I was not interested in getting stuck out in a storm. A small town right on the river called Isle of Hope came into view, and there was a marina right in front of me. I got on the radio and called the dock master, explaining I needed a slip for a 12-foot boat and said the dinghy dock would work great. He asked me how large my vessel was; I repeated 12 feet.

He said, "Not your dinghy, your vessel." I replied that the only vessel I had was a 12-foot dinghy. He directed me to the dinghy dock. I suspected he thought I was nuts. I pulled up to the dock and he was there to catch my lines.

"This is your vessel?" he queried.

"Yes," I replied gleefully. "How do you like her?"

"She's small. Where did you sail from?" he asked.

"St. Petersburg, Florida," I replied with pride.

He shook his head and said, "I went to Eckerd College."

We both started laughing. He gave me dockage and power for free. I secured the boat and we made our way to the Marina Store just as it started to rain. I called Lisa, my hostess for the night. Her mother went to church with my parents in Melrose. Lisa came and picked me up after work. We headed out to her husband's work on the way to her house. Her husband, Scott, retired from the Coast Guard, was the pilot of the rogue helicopter that had been buzzing me. His primary job was mosquito control, and he assisted with local search and rescue missions. I now understood his expertise with the copter.

The next morning, Scott took me to the marina and I got on board to make my way across the Savannah River into South Carolina. The current in the Savannah River could make six knots; the tides in this area were extreme. I had to go across on a slack or outgoing tide. The river was also the major shipping highway into Savannah. Freighters moved up and down the river much faster than I could even dream of going. I would have to watch carefully and pick my crossing.

The waterway took a right turn at the Savannah River, and traveled a short ways east before it met up with Harbor River to continue north. It was vital to time this correctly or I would end up somewhere I did not want to be.

As I motor sailed north, the engine started making clunking sounds that kept getting louder and louder. This was not good, and not a spark plug issue. I knew I did not want to try the Savannah River with my engine acting up, so I pulled into the Savannah Yacht Club. They got me in touch with Lem of Boaters Paradise. He came and looked at the engine, and said the connecting rod had come loose and was beating up the engine. He suggested a new one.

I made a call to Nissan and we were connected to West Marine in Savannah. They happened to have one in stock and gave it to me. I was up and running the next morning and headed out at 8:00 a.m. to make the tide across the Savannah River.

As I moved up the Harbor River toward Calibogue Sound to Hilton Head Island, I could see storm clouds building inland. I had a contact waiting for me at the South Carolina Yacht Club. This part of the Intracoastal was busy with lots of boat traffic. I was once again in wake city, sailing and bailing.

To get into Windmill Harbor at the Yacht Club you had to go through a lock. The tides were so extreme on this part of the coast, with nine-foot differentials, that if they didn't lock the water into the harbor, the boats would be aground every time the tide went out. Because of the coming storm I had to wait for the next opening; they were trying to get all the boats into safety. This was the first time I had ever been in a lock. It was an amazing process and went very well. My new engine worked great, too!

Debbie welcomed me with open arms. They provided facilities so I could scrub down the boat. It was a really special time for me, washing the *Prevail*. She had carried me so far and so well. After I was done, I headed up to Debbie's house, cleaned up, and changed for an event at the South Carolina Yacht Club. The Salty Sisters welcomed me into the fold and made me an honorary member. Today, I still wear the polo shirt they gave me!

Debbie is quite an athlete. She was taught to sail by her father at a young age and runs the sailing program out of the yacht club for the kids. She has sailed all over the world and is also an avid tennis player.

Besides physical prowess, she is a well-educated humanitarian. She taught school at the Indian reservations out west for part of her career. We connected and made a lasting friendship.

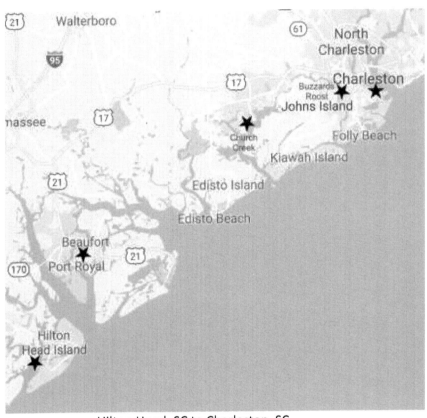

Hilton Head, SC to Charleston, SC

CHAPTER 16

I have suffered a great many catastrophes in my life.
Most of which never happened.

~

- Mark Twain -

Hilton Head, South Carolina to Charleston, South Carolina
May 28 to June 3, 2000

My stay in Hilton Head went by too quickly. I could have just roosted there forever. Now I had to leave and head toward Beaufort, South Carolina. I was looking forward to this stop, as my godparents lived there. Then it was on to Charleston, where I'd learned to sail. Another homecoming. But before I got too nostalgic, I had to cross yet another sound in a strong breeze.

How do you spell choppy water?

SOAKING WET!

So much for the freshwater rinse I had given the boat. I ducked into Skull Creek Marina to see if it would calm down before trying Port Royale Sound. Knowing that I was anxious about another crossing, Debbie sent the cavalry to meet me: Michael on *Pippatoo*.

We sailed out to the sound together, and the moral support was great. As we poked our noses out from the creek into the sound, it was obvious that the wind had dropped. I waved goodbye to *Pippatoo* and headed into Port Royal Sound. I had a nice crossing, enjoying sailing freely once again!

Then, it was back into the wonderful salt marshes. I stripped down to my bikini and started to sing and dance as I made my way up this section of the Intracoastal. As I was nearing a junction, I noticed a shrimp boat with its net booms down coming in from the Atlantic Ocean. There was a motley crew on board, and they started pointing and jeering at me. I quickly put on my shirt and pajama bottoms, then they started waving and whistling.

The shrimp boat stopped in front of me, blocking my way. I kept as much distance as possible without turning around and running for it. I opened the hatch in front of me and pulled out my flare gun. Then activity broke out on deck and the booms were raised on the boat to make ready for docking. The captain once again started moving the boat across the channel up the waterway to their harbor.

I felt a bit of a fool, thinking it had been about me when it was really about the shrimp boat. Yes, the crew's actions were disconcerting, but I had not been in danger. I put the flare gun away and continued to make my way north.

The wind died as I came up to Paris Island, so I started the engine and made the Beaufort Yacht and Sailing Club by 3:00 in the afternoon. I had an interview with the local paper, and then my godparents, Clyde and Betty Jo Fulcher, took me out to dinner.

After a nice night in a clean bed, I waved goodbye to them the next morning as I headed for Charleston, South Carolina. It was going to take me two days of sailing ... er, motoring, as the wind shut off.

St. Helena's Sound was benign, and I motored across and headed up the Ashepoo River to meet the Edisto River. I had been warned about the currents in this area and knew my motor was not strong enough to make against them. If I got caught in an outgoing flow, I would need to put the anchor down and wait until the tide turned. I had been warned that in a strong current with the anchor down, the boat could become submerged; another thing to worry about. There were so many potential things that could go wrong and kill a person, no wonder I had been having anxiety.

Once back inland, the Wadmalaw River became the Intracoastal Waterway and wound its way past Seabrook Island and Kiawah Island, the land of the salt marshes with which I was starting to have a love affair. I also loved camping out, watching the sun set and rise over the marsh. The colors were incredible. The music of the birds, especially the barking of the marsh hens, made a grand substitute for a radio.

I spent the night in Church Creek on the hook, a favorite local hurricane hole and boat anchorage. I put up my mosquito net and voodoo, then cuddled up under my tablecloth and got a good rest that night.

***

The next morning, I lazed around, as I knew the upcoming bridge didn't open until 9:00. I met three other boats that I had been anchored with, all waiting for the bridge opening. The bridge was having electrical difficulties, so I rafted to a big catamaran to wait it out.

We were finally able to get through at 10:30. As I meandered my way toward Charleston, the Wadmalaw River became the Stono River, and I came upon a couple standing on a spoil island with their powerboat hard aground. They were flashing a light and waving, so I went over to them and asked if they needed help. I guess my small craft did not look very comforting to them, and they said they weren't in trouble. I did try to call the Coast Guard just to see if I could, but I didn't get a response. They probably could not hear me. Not very comforting!

It was a short run for me from there to Buzzards Roost Marina on the Stono River. My brother, who lived at the marina on a powerboat, had arranged for me to stay there before I made my way into Charleston Harbor the next day. We looked at the charts and he warned me of the narrows, Elliot's Cut on Wappoo Creek. This body of water is known for its strong currents. I would have to go through it before I came out into Ashley River and Charleston Harbor.

I waited for the tide to turn before trying Elliot's Cut. It was then a quick trip across the Ashley River to St. Bart's at the City Marina. Charleston was where I'd learned to sail, and my, had it changed in the last 20 years. The docks at St. Bart's were floating and new. What a treat!

One of the guys at St. Bart's told me about a watersports program for people with special needs in Charleston, called Anchors Away, that taught waterskiing, sailing, and jet skiing.

Anchors Away was having a fundraiser on that very Sunday afternoon and invited me, Tim Wall from CNN, and Ken and Jill from SPPD, who had met me in Charleston. I was given the opportunity to speak to the group, which was great since one of the purposes of this trip was to increase awareness of the sport of sailing and to network with other programs on the East Coast.

I was introduced to members of the Charleston Yacht Club and the harbor master. I had the opportunity to learn about the upcoming leg, make contacts for places to stay, and rest. It also provided me with the chance to catch up on my emails. The kids asked the best questions, and I could not leave them hanging for long. It continued to amaze me how the trip just kept unfolding and I was consistently in the right place at the right time to further the mission.

Ken put a real compass on the boat, one that did not depend on electricity. In case I lost power, I could find my way! We talked about the expedition. I shared my fears and my struggle with trusting God. When the fears of safety would arise, I would start chanting, "Let go, let God, and trust." I'd been doing a lot of chanting. He said this was part of the process of a survival training in the Army, focusing on what needed to be accomplished, the mission and not on the fears. I was not thinking in terms of a survival mission, I was thinking in terms of making the waterways safe and accessible for people with disabilities.

The next morning, the weather started to deteriorate. A front had been making its way across the southeast and so I opted to stay in Charleston for a couple of extra days. Beneteau and Sailnet graciously put me up at a hotel. I had been offered a place to stay in Charleston with a friend of Debbie's, but decided to turn it down and stay at the hotel. It's wonderful to be welcomed into someone's home, but you're a guest; you're in their space. I really needed my own space, out of the weather, where I didn't have to entertain or talk to anyone. I was becoming an introvert.

The evening before I was due to leave Charleston, I called my friend Shawn in tears, feeling very apprehensive about heading on north. I felt trapped. I had made this commitment. I could not quit because the world was watching. Shawn just let me talk and encouraged me to rest. Joshua Slocum, who was the first person to sail solo around the world, stressed the importance of rest. I was really tired from having to be on constant alert. I was afraid that if I relaxed, I would die.

It was with great sadness and anxiety that I left the dock, but I was excited about seeing the Waccamaw River, said to be the most beautiful stretch along the waterway.

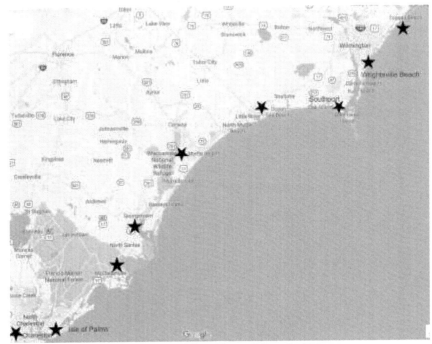

Charleston, SC to Topsail Beach, NC

CHAPTER 17

I can see by the speed you're approaching,
You're in a big hurry to be somewhere.
Please minimize the wake as you pass me,
For on the Prevail *we are already there.*

~

- Rick and Jayne, Windswept II -

Charleston, South Carolina to Topsail Beach, North Carolina June 3 to June 16, 2000

The Carolina Intracoastal has many faces, from huge harbors with lots of shipping, to skirting the edge of the Atlantic Ocean, to freshwater rivers and picturesque fishing towns. After crossing Charleston Harbor with the wind on the nose and a good chop building, I got into the more protected waters of the Intracoastal. As I left Isle of Palms where I'd stopped for a breather, I started to cross an area that was separated from the Atlantic by low marshes. The tide was high, and I could hardly tell the difference between marsh and ocean.

I was filling the gas tank when the cap flipped off the boat into the water. There was nothing to do but hold my hand over the opening, turn around and go back to the Isle of Palms Marina. Bless Nissan, they sent me a new cap to the marina via overnight mail, and the good folks at the marina gave me free dockage for the night. Julie, one of the customers, who was hanging out at the dock, got me a bunk on a sports fisherman, along with contacts for places to stay further along the way.

As I left Isle of Palms for the second time, the wind was back on the nose. I had on my Gill breeze breaker to keep the spray off of me, and my lifejacket for safety. Even though I was in the waterway, the divide between the waterway and the ocean was still not very well defined. Sharing the waterway with big boats was also a bit harrowing as it was too narrow for me to have much room to get out of the way. I anchored for the night just north of McClellanville, up a small creek out of the way of the Intracoastal traffic.

The next morning, I crossed the Santee River and the Intracoastal turned into Winyah Bay. I had a nice sail in the bay; the wind was in my favor for a change and just perfect; finally! I headed into Georgetown to find a dock and spend the night.

There was an old salt living and working at the marina. He came to look at the boat and started telling me about parts north. He said that when I got to the sounds in North Carolina, I needed to watch out because it was a graveyard. He let me borrow his bike and go to the store for water, peanut M&M's, and crackers.

When I got back to the marina, I washed the boat, filled up my gas tanks, took a shower, then walked into town for dinner. Georgetown looked like it did in the colonial days, a wonderful, quaint place, and I enjoyed my evening out.

I made it back to the boat, put up the tent and then sat on the dock and thought about the man who'd donated the phone to the trip. He'd said he sailed for the social experience. I could understand that. I was feeling a bit lonely, wanting to be around friends, longtime friends, not new acquaintances. Sort of like the song from Cheers, I wanted to go "where everybody knows my name"!

The old salt came down to visit me again, but he'd been drinking and started to get too friendly. I tried to politely discourage him. I didn't want to make a scene, and knowing there was only a piece of canvas between me and the world, I was getting a bit concerned.

I heard someone hail me from a dinghy that was closing in on the dock behind us. It was Rick and Jayne from *Windswept II*. They had just pulled into the anchorage and noticed my predicament. Having seen me on the waterway, they'd wanted a chance to look at the *Prevail* and figured this was the perfect opportunity. They launched their dinghy to come over for a visit. For me, it was my rescuers arriving in a rubber duck!

Rick was very forthright in his approach, greeting me and asking to see the vessel while Jayne hung back, ready to call in more reinforcements if needed. After the tour, they invited me to see their vessel. I said, "With pleasure." I made sure *Prevail* was locked up tight, said goodbye to the old salt, and jumped into the rubber duck.

It was a brief trip out to their vessel. She was a beautiful catamaran with three staterooms (each with their own bathroom and shower), a full galley, and a wonderful cockpit. We sat in the cockpit, sipping cocktails and swapping sea stories. They had been following my trip and said we had hopscotched a few times up the waterway.

They'd watched me struggle in the wake of large vessels and composed a poem for me, which is at the beginning of this chapter.

We passed a delightful evening, and the old salt wandered away. I was hoping he'd found a place to sleep it off. Rick and Jayne offered a stateroom for my use for the night, but I really felt the need to sleep on *Prevail* and get an early start in the morning.

Rick asked if I had a handheld radio and I responded in the affirmative. He said he would set his to channel 13 and I was to set mine to the same. If I had a midnight visitor, I was to call him immediately and he would come and rescue me. Sailors watch out for sailors, and the law of the sea continued to take care of me.

***

The next morning, I headed for the Waccamaw River, which was all it was promised to be. Freshwater, with tannic acid turning the water a translucent black. The cypress marshes on the shore were home to alligators, water moccasins, osprey, and eagles. It was also home to every recreational powerboat in the area. They went flying by me. I just could not understand why anyone would rush through such beauty. The speed not only threw wakes that filled my boat with water and threatened to capsize me, but also took their toll on the old cypress trees along the bank. This was becoming very disheartening.

I took a break and anchored on a sandy bank next to a family having a Saturday afternoon outing. In the freshwater, I washed the boat bottom, the deck, and the salt off of me. The family told me about Osprey Marina at the end of a narrows and suggested I spent the night.

I headed on up the river under power. It was once again time to fill up the tank, and I looked around for oncoming traffic. I really hated to take the time to anchor, fill up the tank, and get going again. In fact, I had gotten to where I was not even stopping the engine to fill it up. I would put it in neutral and drift as I put the next gallon of gas in. As I was just finishing the task, I heard a powerboat coming out of nowhere. He was bearing down on me at top speed and had his head turned talking to his friends on the boat.

I quickly screwed on the gas cap, put the engine in forward, and started waving and screaming. He saw me at the last second, swerved, and got the boat stopped. Close call! He looked as scared as I was, and apologized profusely. I suggested that he slow down a little in narrow passageways.

I made my way on up river and saw the canal to Osprey Marina. As I pulled into the marina, the same powerboat and driver were at the dock. He asked me about the *Prevail* and the mission. He decided to make the scare up to me and paid for my stay overnight. I was treated like a queen, with everything on the house.

***

Sunday afternoon, reality struck, and it was back to saltwater and powerboat heaven along Myrtle Beach. Myrtle Beach pleasure craft traffic made Miami/Ft. Lauderdale look like a backwater town. I was glad my boat wake steering was becoming much more proficient. I made it through safely, but a bit shaken up.

Bob and Emily met me and took care of me right after I crossed into North Carolina. I had met their son in Charleston and he called in his parents to help. They rolled out the red carpet for me. It was a wonderful respite after the waterway madness.

I traveled on to Southport, where *Dawson's Creek* was filmed. It was a beautiful fishing village with a motel, store, and dockage all within walking distance, at the mouth of the Cape Fear River. The proprietors of the Provision Company Bar, a great bar/restaurant with a floating dock, provided me with local knowledge of the Cape Fear River.

I got on the phone with some of the SPPD volunteers to update them on my status and my upcoming itinerary. Their biggest news and concern was that SPPD's board of directors had discontinued the community sailing program. I had left the program well and healthy with lots of volunteers. The community sailing program had been the whole point of the trip. So, what was I raising money and awareness for?

I called Ken and asked him about this decision. He said the program was too expensive and they were going to concentrate on coaching Paralympic sailing. He said the money was in coaching; they could get $300.00 per hour.

I argued about the cost of the community program, saying it didn't cost them anything but the insurance. The participants used the boats at no cost; the City of St. Petersburg Parks and Recreation Department and CAPI (Committee to Advocate for Persons with Impairments) used funds raised by the fines people paid for parking illegally in handicapped parking spaces; this kept the sailing center accessible. Volunteers took the sailors out, so the costs were minimal. He would not listen to my arguments. The program had been terminated. I was stunned.

I walked over to the other side of the peninsular. I could not see the river from the marina. There were whitecaps and I knew I would have to wait until the tide turned and the water lay down a little. I went back to the marina and ordered lunch. I just could not wrap my mind around the community sailing program being terminated. I felt helpless, no more able to fight the physical tide of the Cape Fear River than I could the change in the tide of SPPD at home.

The tide did change as it always does, and it was time to leave the dock and head up the river. These were major shipping lanes with freighters, tugs with tows, and ferry traffic that constantly traversed the river. It was blowing 15-20 knots from the southwest when I left. Thinking that the chop would lay down as the tide turned and that there would be a sheltered shore, I headed out.

As I came out of the sheltered marina and turned into the mouth of the river, three- to five-foot seas with a following wind hit me. I now knew why they called it Cape Fear! But there was no going back. I could not turn the boat around and sail into the headwind, current and seas.

It would have been impossible to get back to the marina. I would have to learn to surf, quick! I knew that I had a safe marina and bed for the night if I made it to Wrightsville Beach. This thought kept me going; someone was expecting me at the end of the sail.

I was under reefed main and jib, and glad I had scouted the river before I left and made that sail plan decision. I didn't think I could have reefed the sail underway; it was too tenuous. I could feel the boat rise as a wave came under the stern. Instead of going straight down the face, I would go at a 45-degree angle. This kept my boat upright, instead of pitch-poling. Pitch-poling is the nautical term for a cartwheel. That kind of accident would rip the mast and me off the boat.

Because I was always playing the angles of the waves, I had to frequently adjust course by gybing, which can be a dangerous maneuver. The main boom can come flying across the deck if the timing is off or the wind makes a sudden change of direction. If you don't duck in time, you could literally lose your head. The boat could also flip over.

As I was surfing the Cape Fear River on the brink of out of control, a ferryboat came out of a dock and gathered much more speed than I anticipated. I had no way to step on the brake; all I could do was turn as gingerly as possible and see if I could cross far enough behind them so I would not become a non-paying customer. The ferry captain noticed my dilemma. He could see the whites of my eyes and knuckles. He gunned it and passed in front of me. It was a close call.

The Intracoastal veered off to the right and the main shipping channel went left. I was glad I had studied the chart, as I would not have been able to surf and navigate at the same time. The boat handled the surf better than I did. I had to keep reminding myself of all the things I had been told about surfing; the first rule was not to look back, just feel the waves and the surf. This advice of "don't look back" came from the early days of sailing ships. If the person helming the boat turned to look back at the waves coming at them, they would inadvertently turn the wheel, putting the boat sideways to the wave. Sideways to the waves meant you were about to be knocked down.

It took a lot of self-discipline not to turn and look back at what was coming for you. You had to trust all your other senses, including feel and sound. I also kept in my mind all the well wishes and prayers that people were sending me. That's what gave me the strength to keep going. I reached Wrightsville Beach on an adrenaline high!

At Oceana Marina, Willie the dock master took care of me and the boat. He restored classic boats and showed me a wooden Chris-craft he had restored. It was so polished, I could see my reflection in the gloss.

He even called NBC and got them to come down to the marina to interview me.

Jane (Hilton Head Debbie's sister) put me up in her home. She shared with me her incredible paintings of the sea. She, too, had learned to sail from her father, had braved storms in small boats, and was able to express it in her art.

***

The next morning, Debbie took me back to the marina. Willie met me for the sendoff, presenting me with a gardenia. How had he known it was my favorite flower? I put it in a bottle of water and placed that in my cup holder. It was a wonderful reminder of all the supportive people I had met thus far.

I left Wrightsville Beach and reached the Wrightsville Beach bridge at 12:01 p.m. The bridge tender told me that I had missed the hourly opening and would have to wait until 1:00 p.m. I pulled up to a dock to wait, overwhelmed with feelings of frustration. The closing of the community sailing program was heavy on my mind. The frustration continued throughout the day, ending with a mad dash into a marina at 5:00 p.m. to avoid another storm.

The marina at Topsail Beach was up a narrow channel just off of the Intracoastal Waterway. They had floating docks, a fuel dock, and a store, so I stocked up on everything I needed. I had been running the engine most of the day and was starting to feel like a fraud. This was supposed to be a sailing journey, I was under power most of the time. Tom Casey had known what he was talking about.

The Intracoastal is a narrow waterway with the express purpose of moving materials up and down the coast, a highway for military and commercial interests, not a recreational venue. There are places that are conducive to recreational sailing, but these are connected by long stretches of narrows.

The marina was quiet, so I felt comfortable sleeping under the mosquito net.

***

The next morning, I left the marina very early to try to make it to Swansboro. The engine stopped as I got halfway out of the channel. I threw out the hook and changed the spark plug. I still could not get the engine started, so I raised the sails and sailed back into the marina, glad for at least some breeze. I went toward the office to ask about a mechanic, feeling as though I was moving through lead.

I ran into a wonderful man who came and looked at the engine and informed me that I had run out of gas. This was very strange, as I'd always filled the engine the night before a departure, but I'd forgotten in my tired and frustrated state.

Once more, I left the dock under power. I went down the heavily wooded channel and I turned out into the path of a sports fisherman. I had not noticed him coming from behind the trees on shore. I threw the engine into reverse and he squeaked past me. The day's weather was a replica of the day before—heavy southwest winds, chop, and threatening squalls. Throw slow bridges and lots of boat traffic in the mix, and I was beginning to question my sanity. I was also becoming more concerned about me. I realized I had made some stupid mistakes that morning. It was time to sit up and pay attention! It is the little stupid mistakes than can cause your downfall.

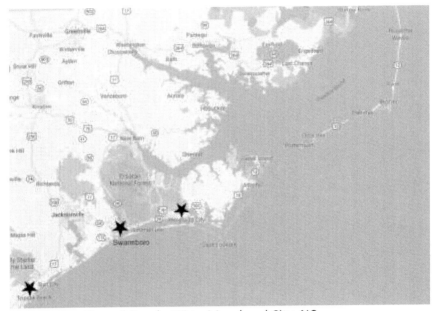

Topsail Beach, NC to Morehead City, NC

CHAPTER 18

I really don't know why it is that all of us are so committed to the sea, except I think it's because in addition to the fact that the sea changes, and the light changes, and ships change, it's because we all came from the sea. And it is an interesting biological fact that all of us have in our veins the exact same percentage of salt in our blood that exists in the ocean, and, therefore, we have salt in our blood, in our sweat, in our tears. We are tied to the ocean. And when we go back to the sea— whether it is to sail or to watch it—we are going back from whence we came.

~

- John F. Kennedy -

Topsail Beach, North Carolina to Morehead City, North Carolina
June 16 to June 19, 2000

My next landmark was Camp Lejeune, North Carolina. It was the first time I had been in the area since we'd moved away when I was two years old. My dad told me that I'd had my first experience with waves on these beaches. He said I would stand at the edge of the ocean in my diaper, then a wave would roll in and knock me down, and I would giggle and stand up, ready for the next one. I wasn't giggling now.

I had been told to be cautious in this area as the Marines ran drills across the waterway, so it was sometimes closed. I saw Marines and military amphibious vehicles under camouflage along the barrier island as I motored by.

I started to question the value of spending day after day motoring up the waterway, so I decided a ceremony was in order. I took the gardenia from the bottle and asked God to guide me to the right path. I then dropped the flower into the water at the place of my birth, a very fitting place for a ceremony asking guidance for my life.

I put into a marina in Swansboro. It was packed with boats, so good thing I didn't take up much space. It was the opening weekend of the Big Rock Blue Marlin Tournament. The winner took a purse of one million dollars. The boats participating must have cost over a hundred thousand each. They all had professional crews and were decked out with the latest fishing gear, gourmet food, and beverages.

Here I was in my tiny, insignificant boat, on a mission to put people with disabilities on the water. My values were a bit different than those with whom I was sharing a marina. I put up the tent; with all the people wandering around, I wanted privacy. My boat was on the outside at the dinghy dock, with the wind and waves slamming me against the dock all night. I couldn't sleep.

I got up at 5:30 a.m. with the wind still howling through the rigging and the dirty gritty feeling of marina grime in every crevice of my body. At least there was a shower at this beat-up marina that had seen too many hurricanes. I got cleaned up, bought a cup of coffee to drink with my soggy power bar, and prepared to leave the dock for Morehead City, North Carolina.

It was about ten weeks into the trip. In the marina, fishing boats had been warming up their engines and pulling out of their slips before dawn. The sports fishing boats had cleared out by the time I was ready to leave the dock. I didn't want to be competing with them for water room. I moved like a zombie on that gray, overcast morning. It was the only way I could cope with another day of fighting wind, waves, rain, and myself.

I pulled out into the Intracoastal Waterway into the wake of a 40-foot boat from another marina that was in a hurry to get to the best fishing grounds. All they had on their minds was who was going to catch the biggest fish and get the pot of gold. I was insignificant in their morning.

"Slow down!" I yelled to a captain who could not hear my words over the roar of his boat's engine. I edged as far as I could to the side of the channel without going aground. I had no other place to go to keep from getting run over by a party boat. That's all it was, a party boat with the excuse of a fishing tournament. A chance to go out, drink, and prove that you had balls by pitting your huge boat and technology against a small fish, enticing him with your bait. I didn't call that sport. They weren't even doing it for sustenance. I wondered how the fish liked it. I was in a foul mood to match the weather.

***

As I made my way north, I thought about those I had left behind. The people with disabilities in St. Petersburg who would not get a chance to go sailing because the community program had been discontinued as it was not cost effective. Not cost effective, my foot!!

Volunteers using donated boats were running the program. What monetary cost? It was costing the people with disabilities a lot more in lost hopes and disillusionments of a broken promise of access to the water. An access that anyone who could walk took for granted. My only barrier to being on the water was time. It was my choice, not the choice made for me by others. At least the anger took some edge off of the numbness and made me feel a little more human.

The people who'd asked me to make this trip, the ones with all of their physical abilities and creature comforts, were back home. They were the ones making the decisions that affected my life and the lives of those we served. By the grace of God, I was healthy and whole. What a miracle. There were so many not as fortunate as I to be strong and healthy, through no fault of their own. We had to keep our commitments; people were counting on us. What kind of society were we building if it was based on broken promises?

I wondered if this was what some of the soldiers felt during Vietnam when they were risking their lives for a cause that was no longer popular. They went to war because they believed in the cause. Now the cause was gone and the people back in their air-conditioned, safe homes, with three good meals a day, were passing judgments on them and their actions. They were just doing their job. I was getting a tiny taste of their numbness. I didn't have bombs, gunfire, mud, Agent Orange, snakes, or leeches to deal with. My discomforts were really few. My enemies were careless, disrespectful boat captains, my own exhaustion, and the dissolution of a community sailing program.

I questioned myself.

Where did this begin, and how did I get to this point? The name of the boat is Prevail. *I don't feel much like prevailing. All I can do is just stay alive and whole until the next port.*

I felt like quitting. I wanted to be at home in my own nice air-conditioned safe house. I wanted to go sailing to have fun, not put myself in danger. I wanted to have a hot, balanced meal. I wanted to spend time with my friends, people who accepted me for who I was and not for being some hero. But most of all, I wanted to fulfill my commitment to the cause, to make the waterways accessible to people of all ages and abilities.

I ran into two squalls with one- to two-foot chop intruding on the morning's gloom. I called the Phillips family, who'd offered to host me in Morehead City, and they met me out in their yard where it met the waterway. Mr. Phillips guided me around the corner to the dock. I was so glad to arrive safely. I walked into their home, wet and exhausted.

The weather report said a cold front was going to push through in the next few days with the wind going northeast. I had been told not to even think about crossing the North Carolina sounds in a Northeaster. I started to cry. The next 200 miles felt as formidable as crossing an abyss. Despair set in. The Phillips recognized this as exhaustion and encouraged me to go home for a visit and a rest until the weather cleared.

I struggled with feelings of needing to go on, as people were expecting me further north. I tried to talk myself into a state of reason, but my thoughts became more jumbled. I knew that I could not get back on the boat in this condition, and I needed to rest. I got on a plane home with the full intention of resting, coming back, and finishing the trip.

***

I spent several days talking to friends, meditating, praying, resting, and reading. I read accounts of people exhausted after walking the Appalachian Trail, and the book *Dove* which Robin Lee Graham wrote about his solo circumnavigation. I learned that my feelings of exhaustion were normal. This provided me with some relief.

But there was a nagging feeling inside that I just shouldn't get back on the boat. I couldn't understand it. The trip had been an awesome experience. I had safely moved from port to port. People had emailed me about how inspiring the journey had been to them. The trip was a success! I was stuck not knowing where to go and what to do next.

I vacillated between feeling like I was a coward and a quitter and celebrating a safe, successful completion of over 1200 miles.

CHAPTER 19

Success is a journey, not a destination.

~

- Ben Sweetland -

I saw my copy of *Encounters of a Wayward Sailor* by Tristan Jones on my uncle's bookcase. I picked it up and randomly opened it to a page. The heading for that chapter was "Resting." In this chapter, he was telling the story of his exhaustion and explaining where it came from. He recommended never proceeding on a voyage until you felt confident and rested. He said the sea was no place for "heroism" and "machismo." He had circumnavigated the world with a crew in an ocean-going trimaran soon after losing a leg, doing it to set an example for people with disabilities.

In his next sentence, he said that this was "baloney"; I was shocked.

He said, and I quote:

It's better to personally help one cripple to launch a dinghy than to hammer oceans alone or even with a few others. Better to give one limbless kid ten minutes of our time than conquer alone all the world's oceans. Through that one limping kid, maybe not directly, but by God's own paths and even through eons of time, we might conquer the stars.

I went for a long walk on the beach to reevaluate the trip, the purpose, and where I should be putting my energy. A feeling of peace settled over me. I had not physically sailed 2000 miles, but I had started to raise awareness that people could leave their disabilities on the dock. I had learned that there was more than one way to reach your goals and your dreams. I got the message, loud and clear. My time and energy were now needed in a different direction.

I decided to cancel the remainder of the trip. It was a heart-wrenching decision. I was letting so many people down who had worked so hard to make the trip happen. I let the people at SPPD know my decision, and they were not happy with me. They called all of the sponsors, including CNN, and told them I'd had a mental breakdown and would not be finishing the trip. I was furious.

My friend and webmaster Randy called me and told me to write thank you letters to all of the sponsors. I was resistant at first, but he was correct; *they'd* backed me, not SPPD. I wrote the letters and let them know I was starting a community sailing program for people with disabilities in my own backyard, as the one at SPPD had been cancelled.

The SPPD board of directors wanted to meet with me alone and discuss the trip. I felt like I had been summoned before the inquisition. I called Jim Myers and he said, "Don't go alone. I'll go with you."

I told them I would be pleased to meet with them, but I was bringing Jim with me. They said that was fine, then called back and cancelled the meeting.

My friend David Cook called me and invited me to Victoria, British Columbia, for a couple weeks to go sailing. David was the 1996 Paralympic silver medalist in sailing. He was diagnosed with progressive muscular atrophy as a child and had slowly lost function of his muscles over the years. He was currently a quadriplegic. He had adapted everything in his life so he could function as independently as possible.

David was getting his Thunderbird 26 ready for the yearly Cowichan Bay Regatta and wanted me to crew. I was in such a low place in my life that this was just what the doctor ordered. He also was talking about us going on the speaking circuit to provide inspirational talks.

It was an incredible trip. David took me over to the sailing program he had started for people with disabilities. I met some of the participants, and they were so stoked on sailing. We got his boat ready, cleaned the bottom, packed it full of supplies for a cruise after the regatta, and sailed it up to Cowichan Bay.

The regatta had 15 volunteer members, who once a year hosted several hundred racers. They had put placards with the wheelchair symbol on a set of docks closest to land for all the sailors with disabilities.

The first order of business was to unload the boat and get it race-ready. David had rigged up a hoist from the top of the mast so we could winch him in and out of the boat. We stowed his wheelchair in the stern locker of the cockpit. For the race, he had invited a young couple who were talented laser sailors. It was a blast.

The wind came in every afternoon from a nadir in the surrounding mountains and swept down the bay. When it would get up to strength, the regatta chairman would say, "The doctor is in," and off we would go to race. The buoys on the racecourse were permanent, as the wind always blew from the same direction. We were in the spinnaker class, and it was very competitive. I had never had so much fun getting beat up in my life! The parties held each night after the day's racing were enough to numb the sore muscles.

After three days of racing, David and I went to explore the Gulf Islands in the shadow of Mt. Baker. Our great crew headed on home. Our first day was up Ganges Harbour (Canadian spelling, I was in Canada, after all!) to Salt Spring Island. As we were sailing, David suggested "we" set the spinnaker. I looked at him with astonishment.

"Who's 'we'?" I asked. He had minimal use of his arms and hands, and no use of his legs. How was I going to set this sail, pole, and lines by myself, while he maintained course and trimmed the mainsail?

He talked me through the procedure and we executed it perfectly. Now I know why he was the Paralympian! We flew up the harbour, took down the spinnaker, and docked perfectly.

I unloaded his wheelchair and put it on the dock, then put him on the hoist and lifted him out of the boat onto his wheelchair. We took off for town and after dinner with his friends, we spent the night on the boat. I used the hoist to lower him down the companionway into the cabin and onto the starboard bunk, and I slept up in the V-berth. This became our routine over the next few days as we sailed through the islands with Dall's porpoises, orcas, and eagles for companions. I went back to Florida renewed.

David being hoisted into the cabin of his boat.

CHAPTER 20

There are destinations beyond destinations, and the confirmed sailor goes on tacking forever.

~

- Richard Bode -

I decided that I had to slow down, focus on myself and my job, and those other necessary mundane things that are needed to maintain yourself in the world. When I was back in the comfortable surroundings of my home and job, it was easy to lose sight of my purpose or ignore it under the excuse of making a living. I tried to take a backseat when it came to community sailing. I even wrote out a list of personal goals, and community sailing was very low on it. But something kept poking me.

I had just been kind of skating along with the idea of a disabled sailing program, not really putting a lot of energy there. The *Prevail* trip taught me to "let go and let God." So I let go. But the messages kept coming loud and clear; it was time to help that child launch a dinghy.

I was invited to Shake-a-Leg to participate in an Access Dinghy Regatta. Access Dinghies were little boats that people of all ages and abilities could sail independently. They were designed by Chris Mitchell and had been adapted by Australians as the ultimate sailboat for people with disabilities. The little boats were catching on like wildfire around the world, and Chris wanted to bring them to the United States. Shake-a-Leg agreed to hold the First Annual Access Dinghy North American Championships. People from all over the world attended.

I was scheduled to race in the experienced fleet. I went out there in that little boat with a serious racer's attitude. Everyone was expecting me to do well. Well, I couldn't make it go. I became very frustrated. The more frustrated I got, the more intense I got, and it was ugly.

I came back in from my race and asked the builder, Chris Mitchell, how to make it go. He said you had to be childlike when you sailed the boat. It wouldn't behave like a performance boat, and that was where most experienced racers got stuck. He said, feel it, let go, and have fun.

One of the organizers of the race came up to me and said that they really needed someone to sail with a 10-year-old girl who was blind, and would I crew for her?

I said, "Sure, if she doesn't mind being last."

The organizer grinned and said, "She'll never know it unless you tell her."

So, off we went. It was one minute before the start and I could feel the race intensity starting to take over my body. She asked me for a hug. My first thought was, *the race is starting; we don't have time for that nonsense*, then common sense prevailed and I said, "SURE! A good luck hug for the race."

She had no way of knowing who I was without touching me. She needed the hug to feel who I was. Could she trust me? Hugging was her way of getting to know a person she could not see. We were first across the starting line.

On the way up to the weather mark, she asked me to lean the boat to weather, which was usually the wrong thing to do, but she wanted to trail her hand in the water. She couldn't reach the water with us heeled in the correct position. It was important to her to experience by touch what she couldn't by sight. We got a second and third place for the day, which put us in first overall. The message to me was very clear. I knew what tack I needed to be on.

CHAPTER 21

Small opportunities are often the beginning of great enterprises.

~

- Demosthenes -

Chris asked if we could house the Access Dinghies in Clearwater for the winter, and I jumped at the chance. This would give me an opportunity to see how the community would accept them. I would set up a community sail day at the sailing center and invite people with disabilities in the community to come and try. A couple of months later, Daniel Davison called me and asked me to be on the board of his nonprofit organization S.H.A.R.E., Inc.

S.H.A.R.E. stood for the Society of Handicapped Achievement, Rehabilitation, and Empowerment. A subcommittee was dedicated to getting people of all ages and abilities in the community on the water. This was perfect; S.H.A.R.E. could have two sailing sites, one in southwest Florida and the other in the Greater Tampa Bay Area. I didn't have to create a non-profit organization from scratch.

We needed a place to store the Access Dinghies for the winter. I called the Clearwater Sailing Center and asked if we could keep them there. They were open to the idea and we put the organization and liability insurance in place. We now had the means to get people of all abilities on the water.

I called some of the SPPD volunteers who had been dedicated to the community sailing program and asked them to join me in creating a community sailing program in Clearwater. Their enthusiasm was overwhelming. We got our "come and try day" set up. One of the volunteers, Mike, had a powerboat and brought it, his wife Sandy and his children Jessica and Zak, to act as our water safety crew. Other volunteers agreed to take people with disabilities out sailing. It fell into place.

Tim Wall from CNN called me out of the blue and said, "I know the official word SPPD put out about you was that you had a breakdown, but there's something more going on. I want to come and finish the story." We had just set up our first community sail with the Access Dinghies, and I invited him to the event.

The event was a huge success. Tim got everything on film and put together a piece for CNN's *American Voices*. The piece showed the trip on *Prevail* and then my ending it early so I could come home and start a community sailing program. I was interviewed by CNN for the first showing of it live and it was a hit. After that, the local TV, newspapers, and radio hosts asked for interviews and pictures of the new sailing program. We had to get our own boats and make it happen. Borrowed boats were not going to do it.

I had a contact with the Paralyzed Veterans of America, one of my sailing friends, Jay. Jay lived on Clearwater Beach and hated to have to drive all the way to St. Petersburg to go sailing when there was a sailing center in his own backyard.

Jay had paraplegia. He was big into windsurfing and at the great age of 76, had been blasting across Clearwater Bay when he had a collision with a powerboat and he broke his back. His only comment to the doctors was, "When will I get to sail again?" The City of Clearwater ran the sailing center at the time, and they were concerned about liability; they didn't want to put him on the water.

But times changed, and so did personnel. A new harbormaster, Bill Morris, was hired. He was retired from the Coast Guard and had sustained a severe neck injury. He was also a sailor. He understood the benefits of sailing. He had gone to bat for Jay and let him sail.

Jay and I went to visit Bill. He agreed to help us start a sailing program for people with disabilities at the Clearwater Community Sailing Center. Now all we needed were our own boats. I knew the Access Dinghies would be perfect for our shallow water. I also knew it would take a while for them to be constructed and shipped to the United States from Australia. So, I ordered three. Now, I had to get the money for them.

Jay said he would set up a meeting for us with the local Paralyzed Veterans of America chapters. He said they had lots of money for sports. We went to a board meeting. I took a copy of the DVD of the *American Voices* television segment that Tim had sent me, and we made our case. The Paralyzed Veterans of America, Gulf Coast Chapter, donated the money for one boat, and the Paralyzed Veterans of America, Suncoast Sub-Chapter donated money for a second boat.

I called my longtime friend, Jorge, who was now working as a harbor pilot for Tampa Bay. I explained what we were doing, and the Tampa Bay Pilots Association sent us a check for the third boat. There was one stipulation; the boat had to be named *Mr. Bixby*. Jorge told me Mr. Bixby was the mariner who'd taught Mark Twain to pilot boats.

"Done," I said, and we had the cash for our first three boats.

One of our volunteers, Grover Griffin, had a contact with a company that made custom boat trailers. He designed and built a trailer that could carry eight Access Dinghies. I was happy to get three boats, but Grover was an optimist and had a vision that more were coming. The custom trailer built by Bill Owens and Sons was finished at the same time the boats arrived by container from Australia. Grover and I went to customs and got the boats in his pickup truck and personal flatbed trailer.

A small crew of volunteers met us at Grover's house and we put the boats together. We made bunks for the trailer so the boats would fit safely onto the frame. We got the trailer finished and the boats on it ready for transport to the sailing center.

Our inaugural sail was scheduled for June 2, 2001. We had invited all the local organizations that served people with disabilities to attend our first community sailing day. Bill Morris, the harbor master, and his crew put holes in the dock in which we could mount donated Hoyer lifts from Lincare. This made it so much easier to get people in and out of the boats. Prior to that, we had been using beach wheelchairs to float people out to the boats and lift them in over the gunwale; not easy! We had just finished putting a lift on the dock when our first sailors arrived. I love it when a plan comes together.

The day was supposed to just be a small crowd of the Sailability committee, SCIONS (Spinal Cord Injury Outreach Network), and PVA members. Instead, members of Pasadena Community Church, where we held our meetings, came out in force to volunteer. Members of the local sailing club, Windjammers of Clearwater, provided safety support. We even had our own "Baywatch babes" who swam out into the water and re-floated boats that went aground. We were going to have to spring for red swimsuits for those two women! Mike, Sandy and family once again provided powerboat support. And to top it off, we turned the reporters for the *St. Pete Times* into old salts.

We had over 30 people show up with picnic food to share. We put ten people with disabilities on the water. Jay Stagg, our founding member and octogenarian, skippered the two-person boat and showed people how to sail. The highlight of the day was when we got a young man who had not sailed in 19 years into the boat with Jay. He had broken his neck 19 years before, diving off of a boat into shallow water. His injury was a high-level quadriplegia. He became very excited about us buying an electric-servo controlled boat so that he could start sailing independently. His face was radiant the rest of the day.

We started basic sailing classes the next week. Our mission was to teach people to captain their own boats, not to give boat rides. We ran one class of five people a month and one open sail a month, hoping to increase this as we got more boats and more instructor time.

Chris Mitchell was ready to come back to the U.S. and retrieve his boats to take to another fledging program, and wanted to do that in the fall. While I was talking to him, we came to the conclusion that we should host the Second Annual Access Dinghy North American Championships at the Clearwater Community Sailing Center. We invited sailors from all over the world to participate.

Nava, a young Australian woman, decided to raise money to come to the event. She was the first ventilated quadriplegic to sail independently. Hospice of the Florida Suncoast agreed to provide her a wheelchair van for transportation while she was here.

We needed more boats for the regatta, and I put them on order. I figured we'd have the money by the time they arrived. Other sailing organizations lent us their boats for the event. I was living a life of trust and faith.

Access Dinghies set up for the regatta.

I have had many moments in life where I tried to control the outcome. Life has taught me different. There is an old children's song: *Row, row, row your boat, gently down the stream, merrily, merrily, merrily, merrily, life is but a dream.*

I have spent a lot of time rowing hard upstream and not singing. The cancer and the *Prevail* taught me to go gently in life, allow it to flow, don't push the river. Life can be a dream come true when I let go and let it flow! I was so heartbroken over quitting the *Prevail* trip, but little did I know, the adventure had just begun.

EPILOGUE

Never doubt that a small group of thoughtful, committed citizens can change the world. Indeed, it is the only thing that ever has.

~

- Margaret Mead -

Sailability Greater Tampa Bay (www.sailabilitytampabay.org) became a non-profit 501(c) 3 organization in 2001. It is still going strong today with an all-volunteer crew providing sailing experiences to people of all ages and abilities. I am so proud to be a founding member.

Claudia Nable, a founding member, is currently the president of the organization and has done an incredible job growing the program.

Over the years, we have received donations and support from the Christopher Reeve Foundation; Pinellas County Parks and Recreations; Tampa Bay Pilot Association; Rotary; Kiwanis; Sand Key Civic Association; James A. Haley Veterans Hospital; Bay Pines Veterans Hospital; Pinellas Community Foundation; Charles Rutenberg Realty; Bay Star Restaurant Group; Dunedin Boat Club; The Moorings; Sheraton Sand Key Resort; City of Clearwater; Custom Mobility; and many more. Harken through Neil Harvey and the local West Marine would donate any part we needed anytime, even in an emergency, to keep our boats sailing.

The lives Sailability has touched have been many. We have taught people who are ventilator-dependent with no use of their extremities to sail independently using only their chin or mouth to control the boat. We have coached Special Olympic athletes and held training camps and regattas for these incredible sailors. There have been many veteran groups who have come out to enjoy the healing calmness of sailing. The veterans are coping with addiction, PTSD, and physical trauma. We participate in the Pirate Camp with our partner the Never Say Never Foundation (http://neversayneverfoundation.org) and Brad Kendell, a silver medal winner in sailing in the Rio 2016 Paralympics. This camp provides sailing experiences to children with amputations.

No, I did not make it to Maine! But the trip took on a life of its own, which is the case in so many incidences. A journey started does not always reach the intended destination, but the destination that is obtained is the best outcome for all. There has to be trust in the process. I have learned to trust the process, to start the ball rolling, to have an idea and give birth to it. Once born, it grows into its own.

Watching Sailability grow, the opportunities that came our way, the people in the community who stepped up to the plate to make it happen and who continue to make it happen, and the people who are benefitting are more than I could ever have imagined when I first stepped foot on the *Prevail*. I am forever grateful for the opportunity!